# The Greatest Moment in Human History

### An Inspiring Vision
### of Humans, Art, and Nature
### in an Age of Change

## Katherine Maria Pinner

**The Greatest Moment in Human History**
An Inspiring Vision of Humans, Art, and Nature in an Age of Change
By Katherine Maria Pinner

Published by Katherine Maria Pinner
Copyright ©2014 Katherine Maria Pinner
All rights reserved.

Cover and Interior design: Davis Creative, www.DavisCreative.com

ISBN: 978-0-9909821-0-4

Printed in the United States of America

This work is not meant to direct, assume authority, or give advice. We are the artists of our own thoughts, words, actions, and lives.

# DEDICATION

*This book is dedicated to*
*The Master Artist and Naturalist*

# Contents

# INTRODUCTION

....................

A few years ago I was traveling for work. Our company had acquired several new offices. In my role as director of organizational development I led the integration team. I found myself bouncing from office to office: Chicago this week, Springfield two weeks later, Indianapolis the following week, and so on. I was moving at a frantic pace and lived out of my suitcase for much of the year. The work was constant, exhausting, and demanding.

During that crazy year of travel there was also quite a bit of downtime: nights alone in the hotel, dinner for one in the hotel restaurant, and long drives through the Midwest as I traveled from office to office. This gave me a perspective, a view of the world I would not otherwise have had if I stayed in my usual routine.

That year I started to notice things. As I traveled it was obvious to me that the world around me was changing, and I was in a position to observe these changes. I also had considerable time to reflect on their significance. As I spoke with people I discovered that they were noticing them too. Some of these changes were positive and comforting. Many of these changes were alarming. In fact, some of them were downright scary.

For several years in the Midwest we had encountered intense summers, summers of little rainfall and extreme heat. That particular summer was the worst, and the trend seemed to be moving toward hotter, drier weather year after year.

Large expanses of wilderness were chopped down due to urban sprawl. People seemed to be leaving the city to seek life in the country, building houses on land that had been virgin and uninhabited. The trend was toward new development even though there were vacant properties in abundance.

Globally the population quickly hit and then exceeded seven billion. Experts were predicting that number would increase to nine billion by 2050 and that the number of consumers (i.e., the growing middle class) would put a demand on the planet that would be difficult to sustain. "Sustainability" was becoming a common reference, and we were hearing it more and more.

There were subtle but profound changes happening as well, things we wouldn't even notice unless we watched closely. One of these was a drastic reduction in the number of bees and other pollinators. I recall several conversations with family and friends. "When was the last time you saw a bee?" "Why aren't there any bees in my rosebushes anymore?" These were becoming common conversation starters.

Then there were changes to the plants and trees. We noticed trees starting to bloom in late winter and early spring. The blooming season was longer with each passing year. The warmer temperatures were causing a drastic reduction in the number of evergreens. They could not sustain the heat and drought. Meanwhile varieties like figs and crepe myrtles (non-natives in this part of the country) were thriving. There were figs in Missouri that didn't go dormant that entire year. This was very strange. The snow and frost would have normally sent them into a dormant state, but there was no snow or frost that year.

We witnessed multiple simultaneous changes. They all reflected a single trend. It wasn't just increasing temperatures. It wasn't just increasing population. It wasn't just a reduction in rainfall, snow, and frost. It wasn't just habitat destruction. It wasn't just a reduction in the number of trees. It wasn't just an increase in pollution. It wasn't just overfishing. It was all of these things and more. The best way to describe it could be that feeling we get way down deep in our gut that tells us something is just not right, a general sense of uneasiness that tells us we are headed down a dangerous and possibly irreversible path.

That year I had several conversations with friends, family, and colleagues. We would agree that these changes were peculiar and even alarming but would end the conversation wondering what to do. What to do…

Out of this general sense of uneasiness and desire to do something, I started researching ways in which I could make an impact. I joined several environmental groups and attended several events related to the preservation of the environment. I didn't know what to expect, but I was an eager student. What I experienced surprised me.

What I observed in these meetings, events, and organizations was an overall sense of division. The groups were not interdependent but independent, each with its own agenda, leadership, and emphasis. The dialogue seemed to tear people apart rather than bring them together. A great deal of time was spent agonizing over problems rather than working toward solutions. A great deal of time was spent trying to figure out, convince, cajole, or otherwise manipulate the thinking and actions of the "other guy." The scientific community seemed distracted by trying to quantify and prove these changes despite the fact that they are quite obvious and rooted in empirical evidence (not to mention good old common sense). Brilliant scientific minds were defending, justifying, and quantifying rather than solving, inventing, and creating.

I was frustrated. That general sense of uneasiness was growing, and I felt compelled to do something more than ever. I grew restless with some of the conversation taking place. Some points of view seemed not only counterproductive, but dangerous. They didn't just have the potential to create conversational distractions or rip people apart in endless debate but to actually make things significantly worse.

Thus grew the inspiration for this book. If I could sum up its purpose in a single statement, it would be this: to affirm each person's rights and responsibilities as an environmentalist and to encourage people to think and act differently in regard to the environment.

The book starts with a declaration, a single set of principles to which we will refer again and again. The book is then developed in two sections. The first section, "Declaration Explained," expands on each of the concepts in the Declaration. The second section, "Declaration Applied," relates these concepts to the changes currently taking place in the environment. At the end of the book the reader will also find questions related to each chapter. The questions can be used to brainstorm ideas and encourage further discussion.

The hope is that people will come to realize, through reading this work (or through some other method or act of enlightenment), the extraordinary impact they have on bringing about profound, positive, and sustained improvements in the world; that they will comprehend their true potential as change agents in creating a better environment for themselves and future generations.

We are at a volatile time. This is the time for unity, not discord; accountability, not entitlement; action, not despair. There is still time if we change our thinking and our actions. Were each person currently asking "what can I do" to perform just one action, it would unleash a force so powerful as to change the course of history for the better. That would be the greatest moment. This is that moment.

# DECLARATION

..................

We stand at the cusp of the greatest moment in human history. We are at a turning point. We live in a time when all citizens begin communicating, innovating, and working together toward the common good. This is the moment when all human beings really begin to differentiate themselves from the dinosaurs. This is the moment when all human beings unite toward a single purpose. This is the moment when we work toward the harmonious and sustainable coexistence of human beings among and within nature on this planet.

# SECTION 1

.................

# DECLARATION EXPLAINED

.................

# CHAPTER 1

# CHANGE

....................

$O$ur planet is changing. It does not take a climate scientist to understand this. It's a fact. Whether one believes in global warming is irrelevant. We can waste time debating that point, but while we do so it's changing anyway. There are many changes besides just the weather going on. They are profound. They are observable. They impact all of us. We can see them, feel them, hear them; we can even smell and taste them. Some are good. Many are not so good. Regardless of what opinions we hold about them, they are all real, and many of them started fairly recently when viewed in the context of history.

Since around 1900 and the start of the Industrial Age, people started dramatically altering the general sights, sounds, smells, and tastes of our planet. We know this. It doesn't take a genius or an intellectual to realize this, just a few working senses and a tiny bit of fifth-grade history.

At first these sights, sounds, smells, and tastes must have been remarkable, fascinating, and mind-boggling. Cars, black-top, paper, spaceships, skyscrapers, tractors, factories, airplanes, aluminum foil, television sets, radios, microwaves, and home computers were just some of the great inventions of that age. Today they appear ordinary, commonplace. They have become "normal" and widely available. They have become abundant. For those of us born in the midst of them, as most of us now are, they have always been there and probably even seem "natural," as in "part of nature," even though it's very obvious that they were manufactured. We use them without giving them much thought. We replicate them. They have become part of our everyday lives, and, like anything else that most of us see, hear, use, touch, smell, and feel every day, we take them for granted. They have become normal, and so the adaptation of the planet for our own use also seems "normal" and "natural."

Some of these changes were good. Some of these changes were not so good. Again, it doesn't take a scientist to recognize some of the problems that were created. Even those of us who grew up with these changes know that there are some downsides and problems that come with them.

Here is a relatively simple experiment to quantify the rate of change on our planet. It does not require scientific formulas, instruments, or degrees, just a bit of empirical evidence (i.e., one's ability to experience the world through the senses). Locate a picture of the city in which you live from the 1900s and compare it to now. What changes can we observe? That is the type of change we will refer to in this work. The changes are very real. The changes are extraordinarily obvious.

# CHAPTER 2

# DANGER AND OPPORTUNITY

. . . . . . . . . . . . . . . . . . .

Change can be both scary and exciting. It brings about uncertainty and oftentimes fear, but it can also bring about joy and happiness. The same change often holds both excitement and fear. For example, many people look forward to their wedding day. They may experience some level of anticipation and joy while at the same time experiencing some level of fear and trepidation over this change and what it will mean for their lives. A new job can also bring about both excitement and nervousness.

These are the two sides of change: danger and opportunity. The Chinese recognize this. The Chinese word for "crisis" is formed by bringing together two symbols. One is danger. The other is opportunity. When things around us are changing at a faster rate than ever before, this is the moment of our greatest danger, and, at the very same time, our greatest opportunity. Most people recognize this. Progress, as in the change brought about by the inventions of the Industrial Age, created a great deal of opportunity while at the same time awakening us to some dangers.

Humans are changing this planet and have done this at a very rapid pace the last hundred years or so. This presents both a danger and an opportunity. With technological advances we also have more time on our hands. This also presents both a danger and an opportunity.

This book presents some changes taking place today along with the dangers and opportunities that accompany them. Each change holds within it the potential for danger and opportunity. In many ways it's what we choose to think and do that makes the difference between experiencing the danger or the opportunity.

Whether we focus on the danger or the opportunity is a choice. As the bride and groom approach their wedding day, they can focus on the excitement or the fear. They can anticipate all the joy the future may hold for them, or they can agonize over all the problems they may experience. This is a choice. As we approach the future of our environment, we too can focus on the opportunity or the impending danger. It is a choice.

# CHAPTER 3

# CHOICE

..................

The planet is changing. There is danger in this change. We know all too well that we, as humans, have the great potential to destroy the planet. Nuclear warfare, biological weapons, pollution, resource depletion, and overfishing are just a few. There are so many global problems it is far too terrifying to document them all. Let's just say there are some real, tangible dangers in our world today. We all know this. We all know it's also very easy to succumb to a feeling of fear, panic, and dread. Just one night of evening news can leave us with a heavy heart.

This is where we have the choice to think differently about these things. There comes a point where we can feel stuck. We know there are changes taking place. We see the enormity of the problems that result from these changes, and we want to think around how to fix the problems left over from the Industrial Age, or we surrender to the problems, feeling that they are too big or too hard. Some of us just give up in a way, surrendering to the idea that we won't be around long enough for it to even matter. The thinking may even lead to a defeatist attitude that goes something like this: "We all check out at some point. As long as life is okay for me while I'm here, who cares what happens after."

Though this perspective holds in it a certain degree of truth, this defeatist attitude keeps us stuck. Even worse, it not only perpetuates the problems of old, it proliferates them. There is another way, and it is the simplest thing. It starts with our own attitude.

All human beings have within us at any given moment a choice. We can choose to be selfish, irresponsible, hedonistic, uncaring, preoccupied, lazy, and unaware; or we can be responsible, creative, inventive, caring, alert, and conscious. It is a choice, and we each make that choice at every moment of every day, regardless of our occupation, gender, race, age, nationality, political party, citizenship, religion, height, weight, or whatever. We can live in the default, take things for granted, zone out, and sleepwalk our way through life, or we can stand up, realize that this very moment is the golden nugget, look around, and become what we will refer to as "an Artist of the New Age." [We will explore this concept a bit later. For now let's just say it means being an Artist (someone who creates) rather than a critic (someone who tears down)].

Let us consider that there are more people on this planet than ever before. That is a problem. It is also a solution. That is a tremendous amount of brainpower, creativity, thought, analysis, and invention. All that brainpower, creativity, thought, analysis, and invention can be utterly wasted, or it can be used every moment of every day. All we have is air and opportunity. We can choose our attitude. We can throw up our arms in despair, worrying about what we cannot do. We can just as easily dig in and do what we can. We can despair in hopelessness over what we can't change, or we can take courage in the things we can change. It is a choice. We will reference this choice again and again throughout this work.

# CHAPTER 4

# THE GREATEST MOMENT

....................

The reader may be skeptical. Greatest moment in human history? Really? Define "greatest."

Let's ponder this statement. As we look back over the course of centuries and centuries of history, there were, no doubt, some spectacular and monumental moments there. A little research unearths some great ones. There was the start of communism and the gradual decline of communism. There was WWI (the "Great War"), followed by WWII. There was the rise and fall of the Roman Empire. There was the discovery of the Americas, the moon landings of the 1960s, the discovery of penicillin, and the invention of the first computer program. There were some moments that have been long forgotten and some which many of us may not now even relate to or know about. This research will uncover events such as "Persia defeated in Grecko-Persian War," "Macedonia defeats Athens," "Fall of the Abbasid Caliphate," and "the Establishment of the East India Company." Certainly these were significant, but are they "the greatest moment"?

Looking back over the long litany of events, the "greatest" moments of the past seem to lack that "WOW" factor. They may not leave us screaming "That's GREAT! That's the greatest moment ever!" Honestly some of them are somewhat ordinary when taken in the context of the entire history of the planet, and some of them don't seem great at all. Some were terrible when we consider the destruction and loss of life that occurs as the result of war. Some of the inventions were great, but were they greater than all of the other inventions? Fire, wheels, and aqueducts were significant, and we use them all the time. Those were discovered at the dawn of civilization. Does that mean that the greatest moment in human history happened at the exact moment of human history?

In defining the "greatest moment in human history" it seems logical to consider two criteria: it must impact **all** humans, and it must impact them in a **positive** way. Most of these didn't. They were local events. They were centered on war and destruction where there was a loss of life. They were political in nature, which just meant an exchange of power. They weren't as much an advancement for humans as they were an exchange of one way of life for another.

Then there were the major religions. Obviously those are great, and there are many of them. Unfortunately, we need to exclude those because there are so many all happening at different times with different followers; it would be impossible to agree which is the greatest. We can also recognize that many holy wars began because people defended the position that theirs was the greatest. There is nothing particularly holy or great about war. All it does is cause destruction and tear people apart rather than pulling them together. Since there is no unanimity as to which is the greatest, we will need to exclude that category and consider other categories as defining the greatest moment for all people.

Let us then move to the Industrial Revolution. There were more inventions in the last century than ever before. They did impact all humans. Many of these were superior to anything we had encountered in the past. Upon further reflection, however, these advancements also created many of the problems we see today. They did impact humans in a positive way but also in a negative way. They were global improvements with global problems, such as pollution, extinction, deforestation, erosion, soil depletion, ice melt, oil spills, and the like. They were great and they were positive, but the downsides of these took them from the category of "greatest" to "so-so." There was the "WOW" factor followed by the "yes, but…" In other words, the Industrial Age, in which we now live, is great but not the "greatest."

Weighing in against all of these, fire, wheels, and aqueducts really did seem like the greatest, but that just doesn't "feel" right. Why? Because the greatest moment hasn't happened yet. We're standing on the cusp of it, and most of us don't even see it.

Every age leading up to this has been a long series of events in which human beings were conquering. They met their needs, fought for territory, argued over natural resources, defended their basic civil rights, and rose above their conditions. They struggled, and they conquered. Though admirable in a way, it cannot truly be described as "great." Conquering each other and our natural world, though perhaps at one time necessary, can no longer be considered great. Continuing down a road of defeating each other and nature in a global age can only lead to the destruction of each other and nature on a global scale. We all recognize this. What is required and what will lead to the greatest moment is not destruction (the act of the warlord) but the work of the Artist, the one who creates.

In society we are only as advanced as the least among us. Had we already arrived at the greatest moment, we, as human beings, would not still be experiencing war, poverty, and hunger. The greatest moment is yet to come, and it is the Artist (the one who creates from a place of vision), not the warlord (the one who destructs from a place of fear and disdain) who will precipitate it. The current path of conquering nature and each other can only lead to greater war, poverty, and hunger. There is a different way: the Artist's way.

# CHAPTER 5

# THE ARTIST

...................

W e refer to "Artist" here in the broad sense. When a person is an artist, they intentionally bring a vision into the world. In that, I am an artist now. I am acting with intention (writing) to bring a vision (this book) into the world.

The sculptor acts with intention (sculpts) to bring their vision (the sculpture) into the world. The painter acts with intention (painting) to bring their vision (the painting) into the world. The musician acts with intention (playing the instrument) to bring their vision (the composition) into the world, and so on. Just like the writer, the sculptor, the painter, and the musician, we are all artists. Even those among us who do not consider ourselves artists are artists. Here is a simple example.

When we plant a tree, we are artists. We act with intention (plant) to bring our vision (a world with trees) into the world. This is what differentiates us from dinosaurs. The dinosaur did not have intention or vision. It acted out of habit and instinct. Sometimes we are like dinosaurs, but when we are acting as our higher selves, as Artists, we are acting intentionally as visionaries.

This is what will lead humans to save the planet and ourselves instead of becoming extinct. The greatest moment in human history will be when we recognize we are, each one of us, Artists. The greatest moment in human history will be when we recognize our true artistic capability, creating, innovating, communicating, and working together toward a common goal, a goal which is impossible to achieve alone but absolutely possible by working collectively. When we all wake up and recognize our capability as Artists we will achieve the harmonious and sustainable coexistence of human beings among and within nature on this planet.

For the painter, every brushstroke has meaning, intention, and vision. For the poet, every word has meaning, intention, and vision. For the sculptor, every line and angle has meaning, intention, and vision. When we plant or do not plant a tree we intentionally affect the sights, sounds, tastes, sensations, and smells of the planet. We have the ability to make it more beautiful or less beautiful, more peaceful or less peaceful. It's a great responsibility, and it's also easy. It's empowering, and it's also humbling.

The Industrial Age was great, but it seems very uninspired to Artists that we continue to act out of routine, instinct, and habit, just like the dinosaurs. We don't want to be dinosaurs. We want to be Artists, creative visionaries. We all have this capacity. Every one of us is creative. Every one of us can create. Even a child can put an acorn in the ground. Every architect can create and innovate a new design. Every parent and teacher can foster (or stymie) creativity. Every one of us can be an art lover when we view a gorgeous sunset, listen to the music of the ocean, listen to the orchestra of birds in our backyard, admire the absolute beauty and function of an oak. It only takes a few working senses to be an Artist and a few working senses to be an art lover. It doesn't matter where you live, what color your skin is, what language you speak, we all have this in common.

The greatest moment in human history will be when we use our artistic and creative talents for good: more beautiful oceans, forests, wildlife, streams, mountains, beaches....

The greatest moment will be when we realize we are not dinosaurs on the verge of extinction but Artists on the cusp of a New Age, an age of immense creativity, invention, caring, intention, consciousness, and responsibility.

# CHAPTER 6

# NEW AGE

....................

W e have come to view the term New Age in a certain context. We usually think of "New Age" music and all the "out there" associations. That is not the New Age we refer to here.

The New Age in this context is the one we all envision deep down inside of us, the world of possibilities, the potential for a great and wonderful future where the planet is still very much thriving, perhaps even more than it is right at this very moment.

The New Age is not pre-Industrial society, returning to nature and abandoning conveniences and technology, nor is it a continuation of the Industrial Age where we keep acting and thinking in our current context and paradigm. It is simply **A New Age**, one that combines nature and humans and technology. In that context New Age simply means: not the old age (pre-Industrial), not the current age (Industrial), but **The New Age**.

In this context Artists (people who intentionally act to bring vision into the world) will create the New Age (the age where we move beyond the current Industrial Age).

We cannot go back to the past, nor can we continue on our current path, which is to perpetuate the problems that were generated en masse during the Industrial Age. Our only option then is to progress, to move beyond, to transition, and to work toward creating the New Age; and we are right on the cusp of it.

# CHAPTER 7

# THE EXCUSE

. . . . . . . . . . . . . . . . . . .

In order to transition into the New Age, the Artist must act. We have all had conversations with people that end with the "yes, but." These conversations originate from the idea that "so-and-so doesn't change or have accountability so why should I have to change or have accountability?"

This is remnant of the story of a smoker. Many of us have known people who smoke. For the purpose of this example, we will refer to our smoker as Chris. Chris smoked a few cigarettes in college, and this led up to a pretty steady habit. Chris needed a fix. Chris liked smoking…a lot. Chris smoked from the age of eighteen. Chris smoked when he went out with friends. Chris smoked when he had an exam. Chris smoked when he was having a terrible day. Chris smoked when he was having a great day. Yes, Chris was hooked on smoking. Well, sometime around his early thirties he realized it was causing some pretty serious health issues. Chris would get sick and stay sick for about two weeks in the fall and two weeks in the spring. Chris was using up all of his personal and vacation time, not for the beach, for visiting friends, or for travel, but for lying in bed, sleeping, and coughing up a lung. Chris had developed chronic bronchitis. Not good.

Chris thought about quitting. He didn't want to, mind you, but he knew smoking wasn't good for him. And here's where his big "but" came into play. His thinking went like this: "I need to quit, BUT my friends and family smoke. How can I possibly quit? I can't possibly quit if they continue to smoke! They have to quit, or I have to keep smoking. Why don't they quit?!"

Sound familiar? We have all probably heard statements like this in our daily experiences. It seems absurd, but that's what our minds come up with, as if our action or inaction depends upon someone else's action or inaction. We all think silly things sometimes. Chris finally realized that the actions of family and friends were not an excuse for what he needed to do. Chris started focusing on himself. He focused on himself, and change happened.

There are other ways of saying this. Some people say "keep the focus on yourself." Some say "be the change." Some say "focus on the tree trunk sticking out of your own eye instead of the splinter that's in the other person's eye." Some just say "accountability." Whatever we call it or however we say it, our actions are ours and no one else's. If our neighbor has a huge car that spews out tons of foul-smelling odors onto the planet, creates terrible noises, and looks obnoxious, that is no excuse for us. If someone else lives in a huge, fifty-room house that has acres and acres of land with no trees, this is not an excuse for what we do.

Theodore Roosevelt once said, "Do the best you can with what you have where you are." A single person might not be able to solve a global energy crisis, but a single person can plant a tree, turn off the water, respect the environment, express gratitude toward nature. Each person can choose to be an Artist, buy a car that gets better gas mileage, recycle. Each of us might not do everything, but we can each do something. Our neighbor might not do anything, but we can do something. We can follow the advice of Teddy Roosevelt even if no one else does. We can quit "smoking" even if our neighbor doesn't.

# CHAPTER 8

# GEN NOW

....................

For years we have heard that the younger generation is supposed to rescue the planet from despair and destruction. Growing up, many of us remember parents, grandparents, and the media promoting the idea that the next generation was the hope, as if it was their job exclusively to single-handedly clean up the mess left behind by previous generations, as if previous generations were entitled to keep doing what they were doing.

Every year we hear advertised through the media how the next generation is the hope of the future when in reality "Traditionalist," "Boomer," "X," "Y," "Z," "PDQ," are all individuals, and individuals act, not "generations." Each individual has the ability to think and act regardless of their media-generated stereotype.

The central problem with "Gen Next" thinking is that "Gen Next" is influenced by the previous generation. The actions and thoughts we have now influence and shape the present moment and the future. We can teach "Gen Next" and ourselves to respect the environment, or not. We can set an example, or not. We can recognize the opportunity for action, or not.

It is not "the next person's" or "the other person's" turn to try to do something; it is all of our turn because each one of us belongs to the present moment as an individual contributor occupying space on planet Earth. In this way we all belong to the same generation: Gen Now.

The responsibility for improving the environment rests squarely on the shoulders of every person living on the planet. The call to action is and always will be up to "Gen Now," which is every person currently living; for who else can have an influence other than each person currently living? Each person in "Gen Now" affects the environment in which they live, influencing the world around them through their thoughts, words, and actions. In this way each person is the Artist of the New Age. In this way each person can contribute to the greatest moment in human history. Each person at every moment of every day can make their planet, their home, and their Earth a better place to live. The Earth is our canvas. It is time to roll up our sleeves and get to work, not 20 years from now but NOW.

# CHAPTER 9

# EVERYONE IS AN ENVIRONMENTALIST

. . . . . . . . . . . . . . . . . .

$E$veryone cares about the environment and has the potential to be a leader. That sounds like an incredibly bold statement, but when we pause to think about it, it's true.

We know people who recycle, who sign up for electronic bill pay, who insulate their houses to save costs and reduce energy consumption. We know people who drive smaller cars to get better gas mileage. We know people who reuse items in order to get maximum beneficial use from them, things like paper, cardboard, wood, aluminum, and metal. We know people who commute, who adjust the temperatures in their homes to a moderate level, who take shorter, more temperate showers and baths.

The people who come to mind most likely belong to different political parties. They may be different ages, genders, religions, professions, and other demographics. They all have one very profound thing in common: they care about the environment.

The old way of thinking was that an "environmentalist" dressed a certain way and belonged to a certain political party.

We can open our minds to the reality that it's what people DO, not how they dress or look that matters; we can embrace the reality that it is the ACTION, not the person or political party that matters. Deep down every person cares about the environment in some profound way. That is an environmentalist.

No person enjoys hearing about an oil spill. No one wants that, and it is unfortunate when it happens. No one values pollution, litter, or wastefulness. Given the choice between a clean planet and a dirty planet, the clean planet is better than the dirty one. It's just common sense. In this way a 95-year-old grandparent cares just as much and can do just as much to help planet Earth as an 18-year-old college student majoring in sustainability. Why? Because in the end it's the action that matters.

Every person can make choices that help the environment and the planet. It is an equal opportunity occupation. When we realize this it will be the greatest moment in human history.

Each person has an equal impact. Each person has an equal capacity for action. "Environmentalism" is not an elite club. By the very fact that we were born here and inhabit Planet Earth it is our calling and our purpose to protect, love, and care for our planet, ourselves, and future generations. The capacity to care and act does not belong to an elite few. It belongs to each person currently living at each moment of human history. When we each acknowledge this, it will be our greatest moment.

Just as each person has the capacity to care about and care for the planet, each person also has the capacity to influence and do the right thing. Each person has the potential to be a leader. There are many possibilities here. Leadership in this broader sense is not isolated to the politicians, political parties, or "activism." Each person can be a leader. How? Here are just a few simple examples.

The leader can be the architectural firm that innovates a new design instead of replicating "the way things have always been done." The leader is the person who plants trees when others are chopping them down. The leader is the person who cleans up the beach when others choose to litter. The leader is the person who chooses to buy the small car when others choose to upsize. The leader is the person who practices responsible and voluntary family planning (whatever that means to them personally and morally) in the midst of an increasing global population and despite pressure from others who try to impose their will on the situation. The leader is the person who supports and implements sustainable design instead of conforming to the preferences of others. In the immortal words of Theodore Roosevelt, the leader is the person who "does the best they can with what they have where they are." They put the focus on their own actions instead of misplacing guilt or blame on others or simply acting out of habit.

At each moment of each day we can each be a leader. We can work for the good of the planet…, or not. It is a choice, and it is up to each person to choose rightly, to choose to be a positive influence. A person does not need to be an elected official to make a difference. That privilege belongs to each one of us as human beings, as citizens, as Artists. Politicians are elected to serve, but it is the Artist who creates. Each person is born with the innate and unique potential to use their talents for good. Protection of the planet is not an elite club. It is an equal opportunity adventure open to each one of us, a calling that unites us, brings us closer together as citizens of the most remarkable, beautiful, and miraculous planet we will ever experience.

# CHAPTER 10

# THE POWER OF **AND**

. . . . . . . . . . . . . . . . . . .

"And is a far more powerful word than "Or." We need to start thinking more "AND."

During the Industrial Age our thinking was "human vs. nature." We were thinking it was an either/or option. This is limited. Another example of "Or" thinking is "technology vs. nature." This type of thinking assumes that one must either progress with technology or abandon modern life to live in the woods. A better way of thinking would be to take the positive attributes of technology and the positive attributes of nature, combining them in a new way that supports and advances technology and humans and nature.

"Or" thinking gets in the way of "And" possibilities. Better solutions are the result of better thinking. Humans AND nature AND technology can coexist harmoniously and sustainably. It just takes better thinking. The sooner we abandon the "human vs. nature" and "technology vs. nature" myths, the closer we will be to realizing these possibilities.

# CHAPTER 11

# MIRACLES

....................

Religion is saturated with references to miracles. That kind of "miracle" is not exactly what is meant in this context. In this context we are referring to "miracles" in a general sense, not a religious context. Here, the definition of a miracle is something that seems impossible but which happens or exists nonetheless. In this context religious miracles fall into this category, but other things do as well.

In this context a snowflake or a blade of grass is a miracle. Though common and ordinary, these are still miracles. Each snowflake is unique. They might seem like "snow," but when we look at a snowflake, no snowflake ever was made with that exact matter nor will it ever be again. No snowflake ever fell in exactly the same way, occupied that exact space at that exact time, nor will it ever again. Every deer that ever was or will ever be is absolutely unique, as is every person. They are all the same, yet they are all absolutely unique. Were we to experience life on other planets, it is highly unlikely that those planets would have the same creatures that now inhabit our planet. The creatures of a planet belong to that planet because they were formed and influenced by it. Gravity, atmosphere, natural events, chemical composition, soil content, sunlight, and many other factors would all play a part. Even if they were exactly alike, they would still occupy another planet and that very fact would make them unique. This is not so much an exploration of science or philosophy as it is a general observation. If the zebra goes extinct there may never exist a single zebra again, not just on this planet but anywhere in the entire universe for the rest of time. That zebra is one of the most amazing things. It seems ordinary, but its identity is actually extraordinary. It is a miracle.

In this context even an ant can be extraordinary and miraculous. That something so tiny can perform the complex set of organizational patterns and systems it does is a miracle. That its tiny little brain calls, communicates, navigates, and finds its way home defies all logic and reason. It seems impossible, yet the ant does these things anyway. That a bee can fly and support its body mass with those tiny little wings is equally miraculous. Physics, we are told, cannot explain how the bee flies. Technically the bee is not supposed to be able to fly, but it flies. That is a miracle. That a tiny acorn grows into a large oak converting matter through what we might call a "life force" or "will" instead of just remaining an acorn is mind-boggling. What is in the acorn that brings it to "life" and differentiates it from a rock? This is what we mean by "miracle" in this context.

The Artist recognizes that the sights, sounds, smells, tastes, and sensations of the natural world are completely original, that the Artist could only hope to copy them or alter them, but not create them. If the scientist had every chemical at their disposal, they still could not create an ant from scratch. It's not like baking a cake. When we alter the planet without intent, we are acting like dinosaurs, completely unaware of the miracle. When we alter the planet with intent we are acting like Artists, completely aware and conscious of the miracle.

The greatest moment in human history will be when the Artist awakens, finding ways to achieve the harmonious and sustainable coexistence of human beings among and within nature on this planet. We die as dinosaurs or live as Artists. It is a choice.

There is no particular art in destroying things. I recall when I was a child my sister and I spent an afternoon building a snow person with our dad. It took us hours to do. The next day a neighbor boy came over, kicked it, punched it, and it was destroyed. Building the snow structure took effort, vision, and time. Knocking it over took but a moment and required no thought at all. How long did it take the ocean to achieve just the right balance to sustain life? How long did it take to grow a tree? How long did it take a zebra to evolve? Destroying them takes no particular skill. All zebras that currently roam the planet today could be eliminated in a single day. Poof. It's so easy it's scary. It would be as easy as knocking over snow.

Every creature on the planet differentiates between living and non-living things. There is a difference between a tree and a rock. There is a difference between a zebra and a brick. There is a difference between a bird and snow. The Artist is fascinated by living things. The Artist respects their beauty and function. The Artist might eat the zebra to sustain life, but would respect the zebra even more as the zebra was not only beautiful and functional, but also self-sacrificing, giving of its life to sustain life.

The Artist contemplates the zebra, its design. It seems simple, yet it is infinitely complex. We can kill it. We can dissect it. We can eat it. Yet once that creature or species is gone, it's gone **FOREVER**. Who could ever dream or create another creature like it? Could whatever force that put it here bring it back? Would whatever force that put it here bring it back if we are so ungrateful as to allow the entire species to perish? It is not a rock. It is not a brick. It is not snow.

Each of us at every moment can be the Artist.

The danger would be in not awakening to the miracle. The danger would be in acting without intention. The opportunity is that we recognize the miracle and act with intention. The human mind is creative, imaginative, and visionary. Like animals, when faced with a problem we figure out how to solve that problem, but we go way beyond that. When faced with a problem, we can **CREATE/DESIGN** a solution. The greatest moment will be when we realize we are Artists and begin making things that sustain the environment instead of destroying it.

The Industrial Age created some amazing things, but to create them we had to completely destroy other things. The Industrial Age was at odds with the natural world. The New Age takes our thinking to the next level. It challenges us to create like Artists without destroying like dinosaurs and neighborhood bullies. The dinosaur brain was selfish, irresponsible, hedonistic, uncaring, preoccupied, lazy, and unaware. We can be like dinosaurs sometimes, but our better selves are responsible, creative, inventive, caring, alert, and conscious. We will achieve the greatest moment in human history by the very fact that we are not dinosaurs. We are human beings, and human beings are Artists who recognize and appreciate the miracle of nature and life on this planet.

SECTION 2

....................

# DECLARATION
# APPLIED

....................

# CHAPTER 12

# THE MIRACLE OF
# THE CYCLE OF LIFE

. . . . . . . . . . . . . . . . . . .

Remember learning about the cycle of life in school? It went something like this. The trees and animals of the world grow. When they reach a certain size or age or accident, they die. The dead animals and plants lay on the ground. The little things that live in the earth and on the earth take sustenance from those once living things to decompose them. The whole animal and plant is used up, decomposed, and recomposed as something else. Its life gives life to something else. Then that decomposed matter settles deep in the ground to regenerate soil, minerals, and plants. This creates rich, fertile soil. The cycle of life and death and life is a balance that sustains all life on the planet. The ecosystem requires this balance.

The lesson continued. We learned that trees and plants prevent erosion, that without them the soil washes away. The roots function as an invisible net that holds everything in place. Without them the ground becomes unstable. When plants die, their roots also become food for the invisible creatures of the earth.

What we don't see adds as much value as what we see. Life depends on other life. Life depends also on death.

It is a miracle.

Contrast this with what we observe happening today. Roads are getting wider. Concrete is covering vast expanses of land. This isn't just happening in the cities. Corporate farms are taking the place of forests and prairies. New construction and lawns are taking the place of forests. Trees are disappearing. This starts a chain reaction; for where there are no trees, there are no animals or birds, just grass and endless fields that must be watered to keep from drying out.

There is no need to be a biologist in order to understand this. If the ground needs the trees, plants, and animals in order for the cycle of life to continue and those trees, plants, and animals are removed, the cycle of life is interrupted. Building one house and clearing one square mile of land alters the sights, sounds, sensations, smells, and tastes of the land. Building one house and clearing one square mile of land interrupts the cycle of life. If it's just one house on one square mile, the impact is relatively insignificant. However, when there are entire neighborhoods and farms replacing forests globally, it's a different story. As we travel we observe this happening. The land does not look, sound, feel, smell, and taste the same. Vast areas of land are changed, thus altering the cycle of life.

The Artist of the New Age understands that ecosystems and ecology are not limitless and insignificant. The Artist does not take these systems, processes, and miracles for granted. The Artist knows we couldn't produce or even reproduce them.

There is danger in continuing down our current road. The danger is massive soil depletion and erosion. As chemicals are used to treat the ground, killing insects and plants, there is even greater danger that the chemical composition of that soil may significantly change. There is danger in continuing down the pre-Industrial road of clearing acres, danger in replicating old building models, danger in continuing old ways of thinking and acting. How many new subdivisions go up each day where the houses are so close together there is scarcely enough room to grow a small tree, much less an oak, much less a forest, wood, or nature habitat? Doing this one year on one acre of land isn't a big deal. Doing this permanently and on great expanses of land is a problem, a really big problem.

We can tread dangerously down the current road, unconscious, uncaring, lazy, preoccupied, selfish, and irresponsible, or we can wake up and do something different. It may seem hard. It seems as though there are no other options available than what we're doing today, that we're trapped in doing what we've always done, but that's because we're using our Industrial Age brain, not our Artist brain.

The Artist sees the land and thinks, not just how to build the house but how to build the house so that it achieves the harmonious and sustainable coexistence of house and humans among and within nature on this planet. The Artist sees and makes room for trees, water, plants, and animals. The Artist uses the land intentionally, intelligently, and creatively. The Artist seeks beauty. The Artist knows that people prefer to experience beauty. The Artist knows that beauty AND function can coexist, that they are not mutually exclusive.

When we sit in traffic we can take a brief moment to observe. What do we see? What don't we see? What are the possibilities?

Today we may not see a single bird or tree. For **miles** and **miles** there may not be a single bird or tree. Will we ever see them again? The cycle of life is being interrupted. Sights, sounds, smells, tastes, and sensations are greatly changed. We contemplate that without some kind of intervention they may be changed forever. Is this acceptable?

We observe concrete. Empty concrete. Miles and miles of it. There are vacant lots where no one parks a single car for years. The lot is vacant and pointless. How did this land look not even a hundred years ago? The Industrial Age rendered these wide expanses of land neither functional nor beautiful. There is great opportunity if we change our thinking and action. All it takes is a choice, an intentional act. It is a choice between smashing things, paving over them, and removing all life on the one hand, and putting a tree here or there, planting flowers, building in a reasonable way, and allowing the presence of some living things on the other.

The question comes down to this: do we take the extra moment to operate with thought and intention, to act responsibly, creatively, carefully, and consciously when building and designing? Or do we unintentionally and permanently alter the cycle of life in a selfish, irresponsible, hedonistic, insensitive, distracted, habitual, lazy, and uncreative manner? When building in the present we create the future. Each building that goes up is a testament to our intelligence. Does the building represent our higher-level thinking? Does it represent real ingenuity?

Let us take a moment to ponder the desert, the vast expanse of sand and wind. Many deserts were fertile at one time. Things grew there. There were plants, animals, trees; an entire ecology and cycle of life.

There is danger in the current road, a road that depletes the cycle of life and destroys the miracle. There is also enormous opportunity. Architects, Designers, and other Artists (that is, all of us) can operate from the side of ourselves that reflects our higher purpose. Possibilities abound. It just takes awareness and action.

There exists a great deal of untapped potential and creativity in the world. The Industrial Age robbed us of this. The Industrial Age was boring. It didn't leave much room for people to think differently. It trained everyone to think the same. It promoted assembly-line production and assembly-line thinking. The Artist of the New Age is encouraged to think differently, to tap into possibilities, to explore, to create, to design, to beautify.

As we talk to our family, friends, coworkers, and neighbors, it is obvious that people today are starved for a challenge. They want to be more creative. They want self-expression in their work and in their design. They want to live a life of purpose. They want to create a better planet for themselves and for future generations. The Industrial Age was okay, but we're ready to move beyond that. We are yearning for more beauty. We are yearning to experience nature.

Many films and songs today portray a bleak and dismal picture of the world to come. They imagine a cold, dark, harsh world where nothing grows. They portray the danger. It doesn't have to be that way. Of course, it **could** go that way, but why would we let it? Nobody wants that world. Saving planet Earth or completely obliterating it just takes working toward one future instead of another.

The Artist of the New Age is not bound by the shackles of the Industrial Age. The Artist sees the potential and realizes the freedom. At each moment of each day each person on the planet is making choices. These choices contribute positively or negatively to the sights, sounds, smells, tastes, and sensations of the planet. These choices can destroy the cycle of life or encourage it. It is a choice.

Some say we are approaching the end. In a way we are. We are at the end of the Industrial Age. It was great, but it wasn't the greatest. The greatest moment is yet to come, when we begin communicating, innovating, and working together toward a common goal, which is the harmonious and sustainable coexistence of human beings among and within nature on this planet, a moment when we no longer destroy the cycle of life but promote and encourage it, when we see the opportunity and pursue it.

Then we're going to look at those films and listen to those songs, laughing at how silly we were to think that we'd ever be so unconscious and insensitive as to ever let that happen! Nobody wants to live in the urban desert. Nobody. Life requires life in order to thrive. We Artists do not take sustenance from chemicals, concrete, and drywall. We were created from nature

48

and are part of nature. By encouraging and supporting the cycle of life, we support and encourage our own lives and the lives of future generations. The Artist of the New Age sees this and finds creative ways to achieve this in every thought, word, and action. We aren't dinosaurs. We are humans. To be human is to be creative, to create, not to destroy. Any dinosaur can destroy and, in so doing, go extinct. We are not dinosaurs. We are Artists. We appreciate, understand, and encourage. It is in our nature to respect and encourage the cycle of life, that which we know we can only imitate, that which we cannot produce or re-create.

# CHAPTER 13

# THE MIRACLE OF
# THE TREE

....................

In the Summer of 2012 I took a trip to Europe with my family. We visited Rome for a few days and traveled into Croatia for the remainder of our two-week trip. Though the trip wasn't nearly long enough, it was an amazing journey. My dad was our translator and guide. While there, we went to the city where he was born. It was beautiful, and it was hot. Really, really HOT! Those of us who lived through it know that 2012 was a real scorcher. There was little rain and a lot of heat. That summer we left a hot North America to experience what seemed to be an even hotter Europe.

The European city where my father was born is tucked away in the Balkan Mountains. There are mountains all around. These mountains are covered with rock. The rock holds a great deal of heat, particularly in summer. We felt as if the rock sucked every ounce of water out of us. While we were visiting, our cousin took us for a tour. He pointed out something so simple yet so extraordinarily powerful. "Look over there," he said, pointing to a ridge of nearby mountains. "We have grown cheery trees on these mountains forever. The cherries have been here since before the Romans. A few years ago all of the cherry trees died. ALL of them. They just couldn't take the heat, so we planted fig trees instead. The figs do okay because they can take the heat better and don't need as much water. We planted cherries on the north side because it's cooler, and there is more shade. The figs and the cherries don't do as well as they once did though...," his voice trailing off as he stared at the mountains in silent reflection, pondering the significance of what he had just said. Something about it struck us. He seemed...sad. His sadness made us feel very sad as well. He loved those trees, the ones that had grown on the mountains since before the Romans. He did not want to see them go, and he was very concerned about the significance of the sudden change he was observing.

When we returned home we noticed something. Our trees here were taking a severe beating as well, particularly the evergreens. The warm winters, lack of rainfall, and intense sun were causing them to burn up. It wasn't just a few trees that were affected or even a few varieties. They all seemed to be...suffering. Some looked so bad they resembled un-watered Christmas trees that had been left in place from December until August.

There's more though. Not only are the trees impacted by the weather; year after year we can observe a shocking lack of trees. In the past when driving through the country or from state to state we could observe groves of trees in the middle of farms or on the edge of farms. Trees separated highways from farms. Trees and forests could be seen when flying from state to state. There were vast areas of wilderness with groves of trees that would stretch for miles. Not anymore. All of the trees seem to be…gone. In our subdivisions many people seem to have taken to chopping them down and not replacing them. The reason is unclear, but the trend is obvious.

The lack of trees isn't just creating a reduction of beauty and nature in our world. It's also creating a dangerous scenario. It doesn't take a world-class scientist to understand that trees are the Earth's lungs and AC system. A tree cools the ground under it by ten degrees. Ten degrees! That might not sound like a lot, but there is a big difference between 90 degrees and 100 degrees in the summer. Even a baby can understand that it's more comfortable in the shade of a tree on a hot day than it is in the sun. We can all feel the difference. Just take a drive to the country on a hot day. The country seems cooler. Why? Because it is cooler.

Here is a simple formula almost anyone can understand:

More trees (less blacktop) = cooler.

Fewer trees (more blacktop) = hotter.

We have all experienced this directly. It is just common sense based on empirical evidence. No science required.

Trees are also the Earth's lungs. We breathe in oxygen, and we breathe out carbon dioxide. Trees take in carbon dioxide and emit oxygen. Again, it doesn't take a PhD to comprehend the math.

More trees = more oxygen.

Fewer trees = less oxygen.

Cut down a tree, no big deal. Chop down acres of trees globally, and that's a big deal; and that's exactly what we've been doing since the beginning of the Industrial Age. It's what we continue to do today. We haven't just been chopping down some wood that's in the way. We have been totally removing the Earth's lungs and AC system. Frankly, it's not just sad. It's tragic. It's also dangerous. A ten-degree temperature change and reduction of oxygen in one neighborhood is probably not a big deal. A ten-degree temperature change and reduction of oxygen globally is a big deal.

Let's return to the topic of this book: The Greatest Moment in Human History. Now what do **trees** have to do with **that**?! Frankly, they have **everything** to do with it.

Deep down every human being **KNOWS** that we **NEED** trees to sustain life on this planet. The greatest moment in human history will be when we recognize this and start working toward that end. Seem hard to save the planet? Some would think it impossible. Frankly it's so darn easy **ANYONE** could do it. It just takes a slight shift in ethics and aesthetics, such a subtle shift it's almost as uneventful as flipping a light switch. It's the choice a farmer makes: to plow the entire field or intentionally leave a grove of trees. It's the choice a homeowner makes: to plant a tree or chop one down. It's the choice a politician makes: to allow neighborhoods to change their aesthetics and architecture to accommodate modern designs that incorporate nature or enforce a view of the world left over from the Industrial Age. It's the choice a design firm makes: to focus on beauty and aesthetics or just go for cheap. It's the choice an artist makes: to focus on the natural world for inspiration or celebrate chaos, vulgarity, and vice. It's the choice a parent or teacher makes: to educate and inspire children with beauty and nature or rush them to a million scheduled events every day, complaining about how incredibly worn out and busy they are.

The greatest moment in human history will be when we as humans realize that all it took to save the planet was something that was already here that we didn't even have to create and could never replicate, something that was accessible to all of us: a tree! How incredibly easy and obvious.

Every moment of every day we make a choice. We can choose to be selfish, irresponsible, hedonistic, uncaring, preoccupied, lazy, and unaware, or we can be responsible, creative, inventive, caring, alert, and conscious. It is a choice. It would be impossible to list all of the opportunities that abound that are related to this topic. (There are a few listed in back of the book in the Appendix, but the opportunities for the reader are endless). If we just take a moment to think about it and use our imaginations, we can come up with so many amazing ways to contribute to the improvement of our planet. The planet is changing. We are changing it. There is danger in that, but there is also vast and endless opportunity. Which will we choose? What will be our unique contribution to ourselves, our environment, our planet?

The Artist of the New Age plants trees. Who is this Artist? Each one of us is this Artist. We are all creative and artistic, no matter how creative and artistic we think we are. We all have the ability to plant trees and, in so doing, contribute to the beauty and balance of the planet. We can each contribute positively or negatively to the sights, sounds, smells, feelings, and tastes of the planet. We can do this in our personal as well as in our professional lives. At every moment of every day we make our planet a concrete desert or a Garden of Eden.

The old way of thinking was that concrete was modern and a sign of our "progress" from nature. The new innovation is that we take our creativity and imagination a step further to incorporate nature into our design, to realize we are part of nature, to acknowledge our great responsibility as stewards of nature. We belong to nature, and nature belongs to us. At every moment each of us can take a step toward having our planet less beautiful or more beautiful, less sustainable or more sustainable, less healthy or more healthy.

Politicians can help, but they only report to the citizens. It is the citizens that create, invent, advocate, design, and beautify. The responsibility to improve belongs equally to each person alive on this planet. At each moment each action and thought can destroy or create, tear down or rebuild, replicate or innovate. The Artist of the New Age sees the many opportunities that exist: to plant a tree, to incorporate trees into design, to donate to have trees planted; in other words, "to achieve the harmonious and sustainable coexistence of human beings among and within nature on this planet." We are not dinosaurs. We are Artists, **ALL** of us, and Artists plant trees.

# CHAPTER 14

# THE MIRACLE OF
# THE ANIMAL

....................

When we think of animals, Noah's Ark may come to mind. Before he set out on the ark project, Noah, it seems, was kind of wasting his life. He was sort of unaware and asleep. One day God spoke to Noah and told him that there was going to be a flood, told him to get busy building an ark and start working to save the animals. Noah listened, and when the flood was over, he released the animals back into nature. We can learn a great deal from Noah, regardless of whether we belong to any certain religion or even think the story actually happened. Noah saved the animals along with himself and his family. He did not leave them to perish. It would have been far easier for him to forget about all of those creatures! It would have been far easier to just build a little dinghy for himself, his wife, and his kids. Instead, Noah built the monstrous ark, put the animals in it, and then hauled them all along with him. Why do we suppose he did that in the story (apart from the fact that God told him to do it)?

It seems very likely that Noah did this because he KNEW that life would be very empty and not much worth living without those beautiful creatures. He couldn't simply bring them back if they drown in the flood. He had to take them with him. It was just that important. They were just as important to him as his own family, those marvelous creatures. He had to save them. He could make the ark, but he couldn't make the zebra. He could build the ark, but he couldn't build a giraffe or rhinoceros. He knew once those animals were gone, they were gone. He didn't just pack up the ones he could eat. He didn't just save the "nice" ones, the "pretty" ones, or the "tasty" ones. He saved ALL of them. He took ALL of them along for the ride. He also took special care to make sure they survived the journey so that they wouldn't be injured. Consider that there were only two left of every species. If even one died, the entire species would be gone forever.

Is the tale of Noah hard to believe? Perhaps, but it seems that at this very moment we are all faced with whether or not to save the animals on this planet. Do we just let them pass into extinction? We're kind of all Noah in a way, whether we believe that particular tale or not.

When we were children we probably read about the passenger pigeon. The passenger pigeon went extinct at the turn of the last century. Did anyone care at that time? Hard to say. One thing is for certain, though. At this very moment there are entire species of animals ready to go extinct. Would that permanently and drastically alter the sights, sounds, smells, and feeling of the planet? Most definitely!

There's a certain feeling we may have when we visit a zoo or a nature preserve. When zoos were first created, the intent was to allow people to see animals they might not have otherwise had the experience of seeing in person. The animals lived in the wild. We knew at the time that the zoo was not the place for them. We just took a select few out to observe, study, and wonder at. Over the last century, however, all of that has changed. The zoos have now become a permanent home to many species. When we visit a zoo we may have mixed emotions. Part of us may be fascinated by the beautiful creatures, but part of us may get very sad knowing that those creatures do not belong there. It just feels wrong in a way. We humans would not want to be kept in a cage. How much worse for the wild animals of the world. It's as if they are being punished and not allowed to do exactly what they were created to do. The story of Noah has a happy ending because at the end of the story the creatures of the Earth are brought safely back and allowed to return to their homes. The greatest moment in human history will be when those animals are released back into nature. Why will this happen? Because the other side of this possibility, the "danger" if you will, is just too incomprehensible to even fathom.

We hear many people say they "don't care" about the polar bear, the owl, the cougar, the elephant, and so on, that it's ridiculous to care about some snow owl in Alaska. Let us pose a logical question then. Can the world really exist with just soy, beef, and people? Is that really the world in which we all want to live, a world in which we want future generations to live? There was a reason Noah saved all those animals and released them at the end. Noah **NEEDED** them. In fact, the animals were more important to him than his own family or his friends or his job because they were critical to the planet and future generations. A happy planet is a planet with beauty, diversity, wonder, balance, and variety. It's amazing, not boring. It's dynamic and moving, not controlled and motionless. We all care about the snow owl in Alaska because none of us could ever make anything like that again. We could paint a picture or create a statue or write a play, but without the snow owl there would be nothing to paint, sculpt, or write. The pigeon went extinct. OK. But numerous species are on the verge of this disaster, and we are at the very moment, the very edge of being able to do something about it. It seems hard. It seems like a lot of work. Noah probably felt that way before and during the time he built that ark. Yet, he still built that ark. Sometimes it's just a matter of doing what needs to be done because it's the right thing to do, because you can't contemplate NOT doing it. Caring for our animals is no different.

It's effortless to be like Noah before the ark: asleep, preoccupied, and unaware. The opposite is to be responsible, creative, inventive, caring, alert, and conscious. Every moment of every day this is a choice. We can do nothing and change the planet forever, or we can do something and change the planet forever. It can be as hard or as easy as we make it. It's a choice to leave a bit of wilderness or not. It's a choice to teach children to respect, love, and admire nature or not. It's a choice to want to save some part of nature for future generations or not. It's a choice to live beside, among, and within nature or not. It's a choice to redesign cities and neighborhoods beside, among, and within nature or not. It's a choice to celebrate nature in art or not.

The greatest moment in human history will be when we as humans realize, as Noah did, that all it took to save the planet was something we didn't even have to create and could never replicate and that was accessible to all of us: an animal! It is so incredibly simple and obvious.

It is important to spend a bit of time pondering the creatures of the world, the pattern on a giraffe, the stripes on a zebra, the fangs on a rattlesnake, the needles on a porcupine, the hump on a camel's back. It is sheer amazement and wonder. We are very fortunate that we are able to experience and witness these wonders. We have the opportunity to see, hear, and feel these creatures. Allowing future generations to see, hear, and feel them is the only ethical choice. Anything else is unthinkable.

The Artist of the New Age recognizes the beauty, value, and immense wonder of the variety of life on this planet, **ALL** life, wild and domestic. Like Noah, the Artist wants to keep **ALL** of those creatures because we can only at best copy them, not create them. Like Noah we recognize that we must bring all creatures eventually back to their homes, not just the tasty ones or the cute ones, **ALL** of them. Impossible? Not nearly as impossible as one person building an ark. Noah acted alone. We have the fortune of being able to act together.

Let us reflect for a moment on the creativity of people. Here is just one small example. There is an annual conference for IT professionals that communicates information on how to safeguard companies and individuals from cyber hackers. Ironically many cyber hackers also attend. There is a huge amount of brainpower there. Some of that brainpower is used to create. Some of that brainpower is used to destroy. People create and solve cyber viruses all the time, every day. It is a cycle based on break, fix, break, fix, break.... Now just imagine all the brainpower that's limited to the people at that conference alone. If the hacker and the developer could unite their brainpower toward a single goal, just imagine the potential! If that were used creatively on the planet instead of just crashing and fixing, we could definitely discover how to achieve the "harmonious and sustainable coexistence of human beings among and within nature on the planet."

If we can figure out how to launch a rocket to the moon and solve a cyber virus we can certainly figure out a way to release animals from zoos and rescue wildlife from the jaws of extinction. Zoos were the invention of the Industrial Age, the ark that kept the animals safe. Extinction was the dilemma of the Industrial Age. At some point it is necessary to rescue the animals of the planet and release them back into nature as Noah did. We can do it. Seem hard? Not really. It's just a matter of waking up as Noah did and doing something about it. How hard is it to open up the door of the ark and let the animals back out where they belong? In an advanced society that launches rockets and solves cyber viruses, does opening the door of an ark really seem that hard?

# CHAPTER 15

# THE MIRACLE OF PEACE AND QUIET

....................

Many people have been to Niagara Falls. For those of us who have been there, looking at a picture of the place just isn't the same. The picture seems ordinary while what we remember was extraordinary. Once there, many are awestruck before the beauty and majesty of the falls. The thunder, the intense vibration of all that water rushing over the falls fills the senses. One feels the vibration, and the mind is consumed by the sheer volume of water, the power of such a great and mighty natural force. The rush of the water fills the ears. One can smell the clean water and even taste it, soft, sweet, and fresh. It is easy to understand why painters have such a hard time replicating it. They may be inspired to replicate the experience, the sensations, but all they are able to accomplish is attempting to portray water on canvas. They cannot convey on canvas the bodily sensations of the moment and the experience, much as they try and talented as they are.

There is a meditative quality about the place. It is akin to the feeling we might have at the beach, walking in the woods, fishing on a lake, viewing a mountain, listening to birds on a spring day, or the sheer quiet of a winter landscape after the snow has fallen and covered everything in a thick blanket of white. It puts the mind at rest. Problems drift away. Beauty replaces stress, and suddenly we feel relaxed.

There is a price to pay when we replace the beauty of the natural world with ugliness, when we take a peaceful grove of trees and replace it with concrete, billboards, advertising, loud music, car exhaust, what we can call eye, ear, nose, tongue, and tactile pollution.

Here is an experience many of us have had. We are out in nature or on vacation. Suddenly it's time to leave. We pack the bags and get in the car. A bit of stress begins to enter the body as we are confined, leaving paradise behind. Now we're at the airport trying to follow the signs. The vacation starts to leave. The logical brain takes over. We're no longer contemplative and relaxed. We're stressed. The airport bombards our ears with announcements. Our eyes are overloaded with advertising. Bodily space is trespassed all over by so many strangers. There are so many scents that don't mix well: the coffee shop, a person's cologne, jet fuel, the café. It's sensory overload. The tranquil sensations of nature are replaced by the noisy, ugly, smelly, cold sensations of the airport terminal and create a feeling of frustration, anger, and stress. We want to return to nature but can't.

The calm, peaceful world of nature shrank during the Industrial Age. It continues to shrink. Will we allow it to shrink further? There is tremendous danger in that, in not ever experiencing a moment's peace; in having our senses constantly attacked by the ugly, the crude, the noisy, the stinky, the cold remnants of the Industrial Age.

It doesn't have to be like that. It is a choice.

As we fill up our gas tanks, commercials litter our air quality at certain filling stations. We drive through a beautiful countryside, and billboards litter the road. We stand in line at the DMV, and commercials interrupt our train of thought. The noise pollution is getting louder. The visual pollution is getting uglier. The invasion of our time and space is getting worse. Everything competes for our attention until we have none left. Does it have to be like that? Amazingly enough we have choices. There are other options to explore if we recognize that behind every action in life there is an intention. Companies are made up of individuals, and individuals have choices. Governments are composed of individuals, and individuals have choices. Once we recognize our own ability as employees, citizens, and Artists, we will be on our way to the greatest moment in human history.

It is a choice we make to allow our world to become littered with visual, auditory, tactile, and olfactory pollution, or to keep it clean and allow nature to permeate our senses. Those billboards, talking gas pumps, and televisions were placed there. They are becoming common and in that sense seem "natural," but there is nothing natural about them. They are an invasion of our serenity. We can either choose to accept them and proliferate them, or defend our serenity and natural beauty. We, as Artists, advocate beauty and nature. We urge our corporations and governments to do the same. We do not allow our world to become a chaotic, unhealthy, noisy, ugly, smelly place filled with never-ending litter and distraction.

The Artist of the New Age recognizes that nature and beauty are absolutely vital for life, for mental, emotional, and spiritual well-being. The Artist advocates art, not as a luxury, but as a necessity, something required for sanity and serenity. It is as essential to them as food, water, and air. The Artist knows that the beauty of art nourishes the soul and that something profound happens to the soul when it is deprived of beauty, peace, tranquility, and serenity. The Artist realizes their power to shape their world.

Everyone has the innate ability to be this Artists. We don't have to wait for the next generation of Artists. We are each this Artist at every moment of every day in each action or inaction we choose to take. Everyone holds in them a picture of the world as they would like to see it, an idea they have that is grounded in beauty, simplicity, and artistry. Few people would rather see a smokestack billowing toxic odor into the air than a mountainside of trees, see oil rushing onto a beach than clear white sand and seabirds, or a long chain of billboards instead of a glorious sunrise. We are each the Artist of our world. It can be as beautiful, simple, and artistic as we like or as ugly, stinky, noisy, cold, and tasteless as we like. There are opportunities all around for sweet aromas, beautiful images, breath-taking sounds, delicious scents and tastes, warm and welcoming sensations. When we awaken the Artist within us, everything we do in our daily manner of living is transformed. We see the opportunities and want more of them, and our entire world transforms in the process.

It sounds incredibly hard to be that Artist, but that is an illusion. The truth is it's actually quite simple if we wake up to our true potential and recognize who we were truly meant to be. The methods available are as varied and unique as the individuals on the planet. Each person can contribute in their own unique way. It starts with our own physical space, our neighborhoods, cities, and states. There are simple steps each person can take to bring nature into their lives and into their communities. To start, it can literally be as simple as taking a moment to smell the beauty of a rose, to pause before a beautiful sunset, to witness the miracle of snow, or to savor a delicious meal. The Artist of the New Age is committed to beauty, simplicity, and artistry and finds ways to incorporate this into everything they do. The Artist is creative in recognizing opportunities and in the development of their art. They wake up to what is around them, see what it could look like, and work toward that. The Artist communicates, innovates, and works together with other Artists collaboratively to create the harmonious and sustainable vision, the coexistence of human beings among and within nature. They see it so clearly in their mind and work to make that vision reality.

They are sensitive to the world around them. They choose art over violence. They choose simplicity over complexity. They choose beauty over chaos, noise, and sensory attacks. They work toward this goal every moment of every day. They take moments to turn off the TV, the radio, the social media feed, the news, the constant bombardment of sensory overload, realizing the adverse impact these things have on their minds, their time, their health, and their attitudes. They take time to relax, appreciate, and admire that which they could never reproduce: the calm, peaceful serenity, beauty, simplicity, and artistry of the natural world. They recognize the miracle of the quiet moment and are constant witness to the beauty that is all around them. When the Artist awakens to the opportunity of sights, sounds, smells, tastes, and sensations at home and at work, it will be the greatest moment in human history. We stand on its cusp and will soon realize the sheer potential that every person brings to the beauty, simplicity, and artistry of this planet Earth. The universe smiles greatly upon us when we admire that which none of us could create: the miracle of peace and quiet, when we realize each one of us has the potential to achieve that "vacation feeling" at every moment of every single day if we just wake up, unplug, and set our minds on our creativity, sensitivity, and artistic vision of the planet we call home.

# THE MIRACLE OF SIMPLICITY

....................

$B$efore we do something we can ask: "Does this simplify my life or complexify it?" Yes, I just invented a word. It is an odd word: complexify. It is an odd word, both in the way it sounds and in its meaning. Who intentionally makes their life more complex? Yet we do these things every day.

One day in 2013 stands out in my memory. It was around 5:30 in the morning, and I was taking my dog for a walk around the subdivision. It was an ordinary workday, and I was taking him on our usual morning walk. I started the walk with a million things going through my mind. There were so many things to figure out, analyze, worry about, and solve. They were all very "important," and thinking about them all seemed very important at the time. As I walked I started to silence my thinking. Call it reflection, prayer, meditation, or what have you, but I cleared my head. I went through this mental exercise and became more aware of my surroundings. It was still the same walk, but now I was noticing what was going on around me. I was awake.

And that's when it happened: the most beautiful moment in human history. I looked down at my golden retriever. He had a newspaper in his mouth. He must have picked it up from one of the neighbor's lawns while I was zoning out. He retrieved it as retrievers have a tendency to do, so content doing what he was created to do. He looked so happy with that paper hanging out of his mouth. The morning was still dark. I could only see the grey shadow of the trees against a very dark sky. The air was cool and invigorating. I could see my breath in the fresh morning air. I could hear the gravel crunching under our feet as we walked. I looked down at my dog, and he just looked so happy, content, and excited for no other reason than to be walking with his soggy paper in his mouth, living completely in that moment. I heard a train whistle blow in the distance… And that's when it happened to me. It was so beautiful I almost wanted to cry at how utterly perfect that moment was: the cold air, the whistle, the dog, the crunching. Nothing was really "happening," but everything was happening, and it was the most beautiful moment I have ever experienced. Why? Because I was fully present and experiencing the moment as it unfolded.

Perhaps you have experienced a similar moment. It could be eating ice cream on the front porch of your grandparents' home when they were giving you good advice, or sitting on a lake with a fishing pole enjoying the perfect cup of coffee. It could be sharing lunch with your good friend and laughing about something silly, or admiring a gorgeous sunset with your sweetheart. We all have them.

Children seem to have them more. They experience life with a beginner's mind. They experience things as they happen, taking nothing for granted and embracing the moment as it unfolds. We see children, and we long to be like that: free, entirely in the moment, awestruck by life. Though this seems to make us happy, most of us do the opposite. Instead of simplifying, we focus on complexifying. It seems smart, but it isn't.

There was a time several years ago when my TV broke. Instead of automatically scheduling a repair, I realized I had a choice: fix the TV or do without it. The question I asked was this: "does the TV add to my serenity and happiness and increase my quality of life, or does it decrease my quality of life?" It was a simple question to ask. The answer was simple once I asked the question. Regardless of the answer, the important thing is to ask the question.

Does the promotion at work add a feeling of bliss or detract from it? Does obsessing over politics add to a feeling of bliss or detract from it? Does running children to 80 different events every week add to a family's bliss or detract from it? Does social media add to a feeling of bliss or detract from it? Do these things simplify life or needlessly complexify it? Today countless people are stressed out by the things they are doing, yet continue to do them anyway. We can all fall into this trap without even realizing it. People say that we live in a complex age. Nonsense. We make our lives complex. We choose complexity. We complexify where we could just as easily simplify. We always have a choice. If we don't like the music, we change the station. Life is no different.

There is a simplicity in nature that cannot be found anywhere else on this planet, and it is beautiful. A hike in the woods may do far more to add to our bliss than a social media stream ever would. A fishing rod, a quiet lake, and a good cup of coffee may do far more to add to our spirit and happiness than a huge house ever could. Sharing ice cream with dear old Granddad may bring far more happiness to our hearts than spending all the money in the bank.

The greatest moment in human history will be when we each recognize the miracle that simplification (not complexification) brings to our lives, when we realize that nature greatly adds to and enhances our quality of life in a meaningful and profound way. The greatest moment will be when we realize that how we spend our time is a choice, when we realize that we have a choice: complexify or simplify. We have a choice to obsess, sleepwalk, complain, stress out, and overconsume to the point of breakdown, or we can let go, relax, create, imagine, enjoy, express gratitude, live in the moment, wake up, and find the miracle and opportunity that exists for each of us in every single moment of every single day. We are on the brink of it, this greatest moment. It's when we realize what is truly good, satisfying, beautiful, and harmonious, that moment when we let go of "more" and "complexification" to embrace the miracle of simplicity, beauty, and artistry, the moment we turn the corner, look in the mirror and love what we see, when we realize that life isn't nearly as complex as we make it.

# CHAPTER 17

# THE MIRACLE OF ALL NATURAL

.................

We are 100% organic and natural. As much as we might associate ourselves with our homes, office buildings, cars, cell phones, computers, and other "stuff," we are animate, just like a dog, a buffalo, a frog, or a grasshopper. Because of this our bodies function optimally when we eat and drink things that are 100% organic and natural.

There exist a great many trends today in relation to the production of our food and drink.

There is a "re-engineering" of food. Altering the plants and animals for human consumption is happening on a larger scale and more rapid pace than ever before. Experts predict that, as the population grows, there will be an even greater need to "re-engineer" food so that more can be produced from less. We have heard about genetically modified organisms, or GMOs, that turn the wheat and corn of today into something quite different than it was even a half century ago.

Another trend is the sale of bottled water. Instead of developing methods to produce and make publicly available cleaner, fresher, safer water, consumers who can afford it are buying water.

In the world of agriculture, farmers are clearing vast acres of land, converting what was once wilderness into what may now and forever be high-yield crops, leaving behind no tree, no bush, no shrub. There is no crop rotation, in many cases, which would allow the soil to rest and even moderately regenerate.

Driving through the country and speaking with farmers we observe other changes. We observe that the field of corn today looks quite different than it did in the 1970s and 1980s. At that time crops were planted and grown in rows. We could observe that each plant was given ample space for sunlight and water. Our eyes could observe a pattern in the way the seed was planted. Today the rows are gone. The plants are randomly spaced and grown tightly together in many cases. This produces a higher yield so that the same acre of land produces several times more than traditional methods.

In order to maximize production of higher-yield crops, pesticides and insecticides are used. The goal is to eliminate insects, birds, rodents, and other pests that would naturally feed on the high-yield crops. In some cases the chemicals applied disrupt the nervous systems of these "undesirables." A very short research on bee populations reveals that their central nervous functions are being disrupted. The bees that would naturally pollinate the plants ("desirables") are affected along with the "undesirables."

There is a sudden increase in the number and variety of non-reproductive hybrid plants. Varieties of flowers, fruits, vegetables, trees, bushes, and plants are "engineered" and do not reproduce. These varieties rely on non-natural methods to reproduce. When the non-reproductive varieties cross-pollinate with the reproductive varieties, it can render the naturally reproductive varieties sterile in some cases. What nature previously did on its own is now dependent upon human intervention.

This is just the start. These are just a few obvious and common changes occurring that we observe firsthand. The dangers are obvious if we take a moment to contemplate them: soil depletion, erosion, runoff, habitat destruction, over-engineering of the ecosystem, corporate resource control (i.e., in order to obtain water or grow plants citizens must rely on a third party). The overall effect on the ecosystem may be insignificant when we re-engineer a single plant, buy one bottle of water, cut down one forest, over-plant one field with high-yield crops, abandon crop rotation on a single farm, eliminate insects, birds, rodents, and pollinators in one field; but when we adopt these methods as common practice, the impact is significant and dangerous. When we proliferate methods left from the Industrial Age, treating our environment as though it were something to be conquered, when we put ourselves in opposition to the natural world instead of recognizing and embracing that we are 100% natural and organic, we may well destroy it. There are consequences to disrupting ecosystems, consequences to trampling over the miracle.

The solution to these problems seems hard and complex. These practices are so common, so widely adopted it seems as though there is no choice; that we must not only continue these practices but implement them on an even larger scale. It seems as though the farmer, the consumer, and the corporation have no choice, that we have created a grand pattern that cannot be disrupted. That is us thinking with our Industrial Age brain, the brain that viewed humans as separate from nature, the brain that viewed nature as something to be conquered and overcome.

The Artist brain realizes there is a choice. Farmers and consumers are individuals, and individuals have choices. Corporations are made up of individuals, and individuals have choices. The Artist recognizes that their actions have a direct impact on the world around them. The Artist acts consciously and intentionally to create a better world.

The farmer's actions directly affect the sights, sounds, smells, tastes, and sensations of the natural world. The farmer is an Artist. The consumer, through buying decisions, influences the behavior of the farmer. The consumer is an Artist. The corporation is made up of individuals who act for or against the natural world, making it safer, cleaner, more beautiful, who urge their employers to act ethically. The employee is an Artist. The danger was created by employees, farmers, and consumers following the trends set forth during the Industrial Age. Moving into the New Age it will take individual actions of employees, farmers, and consumers, the work of individual Artists to bring their vision into the world, a vision that recognizes humans as 100% organic and natural, a vision that respects and advocates for the miracle of nature.

This seems complex. It's actually quite simple. It's the choice a farmer makes to rotate crops or not, to plant this variety or that variety, to level the field or leave a bit of wilderness, to spray this or not. It's the choices consumers make: buy the water or advocate for better, safer, cleaner public water; buy this variety or that variety. It's the choices employees make: bring this up in the meeting or not, suggest a better method, work for this company or that company.

We create the world around us through our choices. It takes courage to be an Artist, to make better choices, to act with intention and consciousness, but the urge to create a better, cleaner, healthier, safer world for ourselves and our children is a compelling vision. We cannot suppress the desire to make this vision a reality through our choices and our actions. The Industrial Age was okay. It created new methods, but it also created a great many problems. We can proliferate those methods and problems, or act differently. The Artist of the New Age envisions a better way, one in which we achieve the harmonious and sustainable coexistence of human beings among and within nature on this planet. The Artist realizes our world is 100% organic and natural, and so are we.

CHAPTER 18

# THE MIRACLE OF
# BEES AND WASPS

. . . . . . . . . . . . . . . . . .

In grade school we learned about the birds and the bees. No, not that lesson; the other one. It went something like this. Ants, bees, spiders, and wasps are critical to a healthy ecosystem. Each one serves a unique and valuable function. The bees pollinate the flowers. Spiders keep the insect population under control. Wasps act as food for birds. Each creature has a specific role to play, creating a symbiotic relationship. These types of relationships create what is referred to as the chain of life. When one of the links in the chain is broken, it starts a chain reaction, affecting the rest of the ecosystem. John Muir, naturalist and founder of the Sierra Club, expressed it this way: "When we tug on a single thing in nature we find it attached to everything else." If bees are impacted, flowers are impacted. That starts a chain reaction. If spiders are impacted, insects are impacted. That starts a chain reaction. If wasps and other insects are impacted, birds are impacted. That starts a chain reaction. These are the lessons we all learned.

It seems impossible to comprehend this kind of balance exists, but it exists nonetheless. The bee, we are told, is technically not supposed to fly. Its tiny little wings are not supposed to be able to support its disproportionately large body. It flies anyway. That the flower exists is one thing. That it is incredibly beautiful is a different matter entirely. Whether it evolved that way or was created that way is inconsequential. It defies reason and logic. That something as small as a bee or ant can operate such complex functions, that they perform actions, decisions, and organizational principles is completely mind-boggling. That is what we refer to as the miracle of bees and wasps.

People are noticing a reduction in the number of bees and other pollinators. What is causing this? Perhaps it is the pesticides that are sprayed on lawns to keep them looking picture perfect. Perhaps it is the warmer summers, temperatures climbing into the "record high" category for several years in a row. Perhaps it is the increase in the quantity and variety of non-reproductive plants. Perhaps it is the enormous distance they must fly in order to gather pollen. Perhaps it is an increase in air pollution. These are just a few noticeable factors. It would be difficult to say for certain, since we are not bees. It is also likely that all of these factors may be contributing to some extent. Regardless of the exact causes, the fact remains that though there are flowers, we observe significantly fewer bees.

As we think back to the grade school lesson there is definitely a danger in the bees and wasps of the earth disappearing. There is a chain that is interrupted that none of us can fully comprehend and that we could not reproduce. That is a huge danger. If there is something bad happening to bees and wasps, these things will definitely have an effect on every other creature, including humans. If chemicals, heat, and pollution affect bees, they certainly affect humans. We are all part of the same system. To add to this, if bees are not collecting pollen, there are a great many plants and flowers not getting pollinated, which means far fewer plants and food. The disappearance of pollinators definitely has an effect on us as we connect it with the food we eat. Their sudden disappearance is a danger.

With danger comes opportunity. We are changing the planet in some ways that are disruptive to insects, bees, and wasps. We could just as easily change the planet to encourage insects, bees, and wasps. It sounds like a huge, complex problem with a huge, complex solution. It isn't. It's very simple. Every person can take actions that have a significant impact toward the betterment of the planet, themselves, their pets, and future generations. Every moment of every day we can contribute to the worst moment (when all insects disappear) or the greatest moment in human history. It is a matter of choice.

It is a choice to plant native flowers and trees. It is a choice to plant fruit trees. It is a choice to refrain from using harsh chemicals, pesticides, and insecticides. It is a choice to plant a garden or nature habitat. Such choices don't just impact pollinators, they directly impact the lives of humans. Just think how healthy and beautiful our neighborhoods and cities could be, not just in the current age, but for future generations as well. When we plant a tree or nature habitat we create a legacy, something beautiful, creative, and artistic to be enjoyed and appreciated for generations. There may be no greater gift to the world than that.

There is tremendous value in these choices. Every moment of every day every person can contribute to making the world less beautiful/less sustainable or more beautiful/more sustainable. It is a choice we make. We can ignore the vital role that insects play, that critical link that holds together the chain of life. We can just as easily value these things as precious gifts and miracles.

The potential exists for each person to be incredibly responsible, creative, inventive, caring, alert, and conscious when it comes to ourselves and our stewardship of nature. People have such a great capacity to do good, make a difference, and change the course of history that it's astonishing. When a person plants a garden they are creating a legacy and demonstrating their capacity to be creative, to care about the environment in which they live. They are asserting their life's calling as an Artist. As an Artist they affect the sights, sounds, sensations, smells, and tastes of the world around them, creating their vision in the world. The greatest moment in human history will be when we each recognize our own ability as Artists, shaping and preserving our world in a way that makes it more beautiful, more sustainable, more functional, more natural. Each moment of each day each person is given the opportunity to embrace the miracle and live out their calling in their work toward the harmonious and sustainable coexistence of human beings among and within nature on this planet.

# CHAPTER 19

# THE MIRACLE OF
# A SUSTAINABLE CLIMATE

....................

Many of us may remember the model solar systems we built in grade school. The solar system had the sun at its center with the nine planets circling it. At that age we learned about the Earth and how its rotation around the sun created the four seasons that we experience. We also learned how those seasons, combined with a stable climate, contribute to sustaining life on our planet.

It is amazing. How can our planet have been positioned in exactly the right place in exactly the right way at exactly the right angle with exactly the right kind of elements to make this happen and then have evolved over time in just the right way to create the variety of life-forms we see today? Whether they were created or evolved it is a miracle. As we reflect on the infinite void that is space, Earth is very special. It is a beautiful exception to the vast expansive emptiness, darkness, and silence of the rest of the universe. Perhaps there could be life on other planets. Then those are exceptions and miracles as well. They in no way detract from how special and miraculous planet Earth is. Even today we have not been able to locate other life "out there." Perhaps it's for the best. Perhaps we must undergo the lesson of developing greater sensitivity, compassion, and care for our own precious planet and ourselves before we encounter life in other galaxies.

Earth is a true marvel, a blue-green globe of diverse life. We belong to this planet, and this planet belongs to us. We can also feel a connection with the rest of the solar system: the sun that provides light, heat, and gravitational pull; the beautiful moon that changes the currents of the ocean; and the other planets, each with its own unique beauty and personality, creating just the right gravity and motion to keep it all going. It seems impossible that it all happened in just the right way to keep it all going, but it all kept going anyway. Yes. It is, in fact, a miracle.

There is a cycle to our seasons in Missouri. In the winter it gets around -10° to around 40°F. In spring it's around 30° to 70°F. In summer it's about 70° to100°F. In fall it's around 40° to70°F. One season changes gradually to the next. It is clear when we move from one season to the next. The plants and animals rely on this gradual change. It signals to them when to migrate, when to bloom, when to hibernate, so that they can stay alive, so that they do not freeze, starve, or overheat.

Most of us learned such lessons in grade school. We learned that the gentle climate of the Earth is absolutely necessary to sustain life. The seasons play a very important role in nature, and, because we are part of nature and depend on it, they are important to us too.

Many of us have noticed this all changing rather recently. We have started to observe things happening that we never read about in history, things that seem out of sync with what our teachers told us, things we never heard of or observed before. People in different parts of the world are experiencing them as well. The best way we can describe it is that the Earth's thermostat seems to be broken. Weird things are happening. It doesn't take a nuclear physicist or a microbiologist to pick up on it. These changes are obvious and observable. There are armadillos in Missouri. People are driving convertibles in January with their roofs open to the winter air. It doesn't rain in Missouri for months when it used to rain at least a couple of times a week. Trees start blooming in what is supposed to be winter. People are going to the lake in September. The planting zone in Missouri has changed over the last decade so that you can now grow plants here that have never grown here before. The temperature can hit 70 any time during spring, fall, or winter. People wear shorts any time of year. In other words, something's not right. Something's different. Most people are observing these types of changes, and it is not generally giving anyone an easy feeling about what may be coming next as the climate no longer seems as predictable and stable as it once was.

Out of everything mentioned in this book, a disruption in climate and in our seasons is the most dangerous because it throws the whole planet out of sync.

There is a great debate about this topic. The usual dialogue has three main points:

- Is it real?
- What caused it?
- How do we fix it?

Let us abandon that repetitive dialogue for a moment to embark on a different level of discourse. Let us completely abandon the endless debate to engage and discover our common purpose.

We love this planet. It is important to us. The seasons are important to us and to the planet. We want to see planet Earth not just survive but thrive, not just for ourselves in our lifetimes but for all generations in the future. So let us ask these questions. Is a huge truck pumping thick black smoke into the air we breathe the best we can do? Is burning coal the best we can do? Is nuclear power really the best we can do for ourselves, the environment, and the planet we all know and love? We were doing these things at the beginning and end of the last century. We knew we didn't want to. We knew it was bad for us and the environment. We knew it was a short-term set of actions that lead to an undesirable set of outcomes. There is no particular invention or creativity in continuing to do it. It's the residual thinking invented in the last century, the Industrial Age. Given a choice few people would assert that we should continue pumping toxins into the air. It seems incomprehensible that civilization can launch a rocket to the moon but can't figure out a better energy source than coal. We have more scientists today than ever before. Just think of all that brainpower. Were that type of thinking channeled in a responsible, creative, inventive, caring, and conscious manner; were it channeled into creating better methods, not necessarily to avoid a crisis, but just because it's the right thing to do; were it channeled into inventing solutions instead of being mired down in endless debate, just think of what might be possible. There's so much potential for innovation and creativity here it is astounding. Who is the next Albert Einstein, Nikola Tesla, or Marie Curie? It is a choice to be creative and inventive. Every day at every moment we can do what we have always done because it's convenient, habitual, and effortless, or we can break with conformity to use our artistic talents to create something better.

This is not limited to the sciences either. There is a HUGE amount of untapped creative talent in this world. It is this human potential, not coal, gas, or nuclear, that will be our single most valuable resource when used for good.

There are mechanical, scientific, artistic, architectural, structural talents out there completely untapped and waiting to be explored. There are everyday actions each person can take to make a difference. The teenager can litter the beach or clean it up. The parent and teacher can educate their child to respect the environment and love the planet or to exploit it. The artist can choose to capture the beauty of the planet or celebrate chaos, vulgarity, death, and vice. The journalist can celebrate success or advertise failure. The chemist can invent the cure or the biological weapon. The homeowner can consume selfishly or conserve wisely. It is a choice, and at every moment of every day every person on the planet makes a decision on how to spend their time, talent, and treasure. We do so regardless of where we live or who we are. We may appear different, but in this we are all the same. Our cumulative effect can be loving, caring, responsible, creative, inventive, helpful, and conscious, or it can be disastrous when we act selfishly, irresponsibly, hedonistically, uncaringly, lazily, and unaware. We can ignore our potential and our calling to be good stewards, or we can love our planet every moment of every day through every action we take. It's not going to happen overnight, but if we commit to it now and start moving in that direction, that's enough. There's no such thing as perfection. Humans were not created and/or did not evolve to be perfect. The important thing is to make progress and keep going, not stagnating in our old ways, locking ourselves to the inventions of the past, limiting ourselves to the inventions of the Industrial Age, the philosophy of which was "human vs. nature." "Humans within and among nature" is a much more noble goal. We are not dinosaurs after all. Dinosaurs just kept doing what they always did. In that way they drove themselves into extinction. They lacked the creativity, ingenuity, responsibility, care, and consciousness to act any other way. The great distinction of humans is that we are capable of acting with intention and that we are capable of invention. The greatest moment in human history will be when we begin to love this planet in a greater way than we ever have before, when we start communicating, innovating, and working together for the common good, the good of the planet, and the good of each other, not just those currently living but future generations as well.

When we act, we do so with intention. Burning coal or inventing something new is a choice. Throwing litter on the beach or cleaning it up is a choice. Topping trees instead of pruning them is a choice. Deforestation instead of conservation is a choice. Overpopulation and the countless sorrows it brings instead of responsible voluntary family planning is a choice. Overconsumption instead of moderation is a choice. We can be selfish, irresponsible, hedonistic, uncaring, preoccupied, lazy, and unaware in our actions, unaware of our use of resources, unaware of our impact on the environment, ourselves, and our children. We also have the tremendous capacity to be responsible, creative, inventive, caring, alert, and conscious.

All people love the planet. All people, regardless of who or where they are, feel a special and profound connection with it. The greatest moment in human history will be when we affirm that love and begin working toward the harmonious and sustainable coexistence of human beings among and within nature on this planet. We are on the cusp of it, of getting our seasons back, of experiencing the miracle of winter, spring, summer, and fall again. We are not dinosaurs. We are humans, and humans love their planet, their sisters, their brothers, and their children.

We are the Artists of the New Age, a global age when we all recognize the impact we have on each other and the planet, an age when we start doing the right thing for no other reason than it's the right thing to do, an age when we start fulfilling our purpose, our calling, an age when we start living up to our true potential as humans and as stewards of the best planet we have ever or will ever know.

CHAPTER 20

# THE MIRACLE OF
# THE SENSES

..................

There is something special that happens when we show up and are fully present to another person that doesn't happen when we are emailing and texting. We experience that person through our senses. We see them, hear them, touch them, smell them, and "feel" them. In this way the encounter is real. A few words from the person across from us can "say" infinitely more than a 20 page email. It seems impossible, yet it is true. Presence has extraordinary value because it is rooted in the experiences of the senses (how we take in information about the world). The more senses we engage, the more real and meaningful the experience. The opposite is also true. The fewer senses we engage, the less real and meaningful the experience.

The Industrial Age was very good at cutting us off from many of our most valuable sensual experiences. In fact, there are many people today who survive in a sort of modern sensory deprivation/overload chamber. That sounds like a massive contradiction. How is that possible? How can we simultaneously desensitize and overstimulate our senses? What do we mean by this? Here is an example many of us have experienced and may, even now, be living.

We wake up to the television. We hear bad news. Now we're worried and in a bad mood. We get the computer out and start checking email and social feeds right away. We drink coffee, pat the dog's head, and get ready without any conscious effort. We get in the car and drive to work with the radio blaring, hoping the other drivers will get out of the way since we're late from having zoned out on the news for so long. Now we're at work. We're inundated with email, questions, phone calls, and voice messages, having to monitor the work computer, smartphone, desk phone, mailbox, and more. The more we get done, the more work we seem to have. Now it's way past 5:00. The business of the day made it pass by without any awareness, and we're working way past quitting time. We don't really eat. Who has time for that anymore? We're so hungry we pick up whatever is fast and cheap on the way home. When we get home, the TV comes on, and we continue to monitor and reply to our many electronic devices. This goes on late into the night. For some reason now we have trouble falling asleep. There seems to be so much to do, and we are so worried about what tomorrow will bring. We doze off late, wake up tired the next day, and repeat this pattern over and over. It feels like we have no life, but we don't know what else to do. We try to get more of a life, so we create more things to do, thus perpetuating and reinforcing this vicious cycle.

Sound familiar? Even if this doesn't describe our current experience, we all know people who are caught up in this paradigm. They are living with all the conveniences of modern life, and yet life still seems highly unsatisfying. They are living in the sensory deprivation/overload chamber.

The greatest moment in human history will be when we wake up from the sensory deprivation/overload chamber to experience life through our five senses.

The world around us allows us to experience the fullness of life through our senses, and our senses allow us to experience the fullness of life around us. What does that mean? The color blue exists, and we can see the color blue. The rose has a scent, and we are able to experience that scent. The violin plays a note, and we are able to hear that note. The world around us was shaped for us, and we for it. There is a profound connection between humans (and all living things for that matter) and the environment. When we isolate ourselves from the natural world in which and for which we were meant to live and, instead, plug ourselves into visual, auditory, and sensory overload, the stress creates constant mental and physical activity that is in no way real. The modern sensory deprivation/overload chamber both engages the senses and dulls the senses. The miracle will be when we wake up and begin living again as physical beings for and within the world in which we were meant to live. Our senses are a miracle and the fact that the world around us provides sensory input is also a miracle. The greatest moment in human history will be when we experience the miracle of the world through our senses again.

The world is full of so many beautiful sensory experiences. Here are just a few: the smell of coffee brewing, the sweet taste of a fresh orange, the smell of saltwater, a harvest moon in the autumn sky, a cool crisp breeze on a spring morning, the intense quiet of a deep snow, a tight hug from a child, the sound of the orchestra warming up, the feeling of sand during a walk on the beach, soft puppy fur, the smell of a Linden tree in bloom, the sound of leaves crunching underfoot in the fall... The list goes on and on. Each of us has our own special list of sensory experiences that bring immense joy. Being 100% alive means being present to the miracle of them at every moment.

Even those of us who may have some of our senses obstructed can still experience the world. It is a choice. We can zone out to our senses or be present to them. At each moment of each day each person has a choice. We can take a brief moment each day to smell the roses, embrace the hug, feel and appreciate the warm water, see the sunset..., or not.

The world of science fiction gives us an excellent illustration of the miracle of the senses. One of the objects taken from science fiction is a machine that replicates "experiences." The space traveler gets into a special chamber to "experience" a sunset, time with their loved one, a delicious steak, the beach, etc. They could have just stayed back on planet Earth and been nice to the planet and to each other. They didn't. They created a spaceship to go nowhere in particular and then invented a machine so they could experience the experience without actually experiencing anything at all. This points out the absolute necessity of experiencing life through the senses. As we watch those films, can we imagine being in space without being able to see, hear, taste, touch, and smell anything beautiful? How lonely, sad, and vacant would our lives feel without any sensory experiences other than a metal ship? There is a place on planet Earth where we put people so that they cannot see, hear, taste, touch, or smell anything of beauty, where they become sad and lonely. It is called prison. Some might even say that prison would be better than space. At least there is some feeling of safety and protection, knowing that there is still a planet under one's feet and that there is air to breathe.

There is tremendous danger in the desensitization that accompanies "modern life," the desensitization that creates the sensory deprivation/overload chamber, which dulls the senses and puts us in a sort of self-imposed solitary confinement. Extreme stress and loneliness are not a preferred state for animate beings. They bring about a whole host of social dysfunction. There is extreme danger when we quit being grateful, engaged, awake, curious, wonderstruck, and present to each other. It seems incredibly hard to change "modern life," to make it more satisfying. It's actually quite simple, so simple, in fact, that a two-year-old child can do it (and most two-year-olds do it better than most grown-ups). It's as easy as flipping a light switch, and each one of us on the planet, regardless of who we are or where we live, has the capacity to do it. Each of us possesses the ability to witness and experience the miracle of being fully present to other people, to our senses, and to the world in which and for which we live.

The Artist is a keen observer of life. The literary Artist watches and listens to people. The musical Artist opens an attentive ear to the music around them. The pictorial Artists reflects on the subtle textures and colors and lines of their subject. The culinary Artist savors every spice. Artists are awake, alert, and engaged.

They experience life fully through the senses. They both create art and appreciate art. The greatest moment in human history is also the most simple, that tiny moment when each person on the planet experiences profound gratitude for the beauty and artistry that is available to each of us through the miracle of the senses, when we, with the simplicity of a two-year-old child, realize we have the great capacity to live 100% in each moment every day of our lives.

# CHAPTER 21

# THE MIRACLE OF CONSCIENCE

....................

Something amazing happens at a Seabird Sanctuary in Florida and at many other bird sanctuaries as well. Every day around 5:00 in the evening, birds, particularly pelicans, flock from all around to congregate on the wires and netting that surround the sanctuary. The sanctuary houses injured birds and functions as a kind of bird hospital. It becomes active, animated, and noisy as the birds inside the sanctuary interact with the birds on the outside.

Equally amazing is the African elephant. When a member of the herd dies, the elephant herd returns to the place where the elephant died. Year after year, and often to its own peril, the herd returns. The members of the herd pick up the bones of the dead animal, touching them, mulling them over, as if in remembrance, as if in mourning, as if they are visiting a loved one.

Then there's Teddy, a fun-loving golden retriever, a real gentle spirit. Teddy has yet to meet a person or dog he didn't like, even the dogs and people who don't appear to like Teddy. He is eager to meet and make friends with everyone. There are people who told Teddy to "get away!" Angry dogs have approached him barking, and yet Teddy wags his tail eager to meet them, believing they have an intent to be friends, and, as many dogs have a tendency to do, viewing every four-legged creature as another dog regardless of outward appearance.

We can learn a great deal from nature.

There are seven billion people on the planet today. **Seven billion**. That number is expected to grow to nine billion by 2050. Whether by divine intervention or evolutionary causes, we are evidently the most evolved stewards on the planet. Are we behaving thus? More importantly, are we capable of behaving better? In pondering these questions some people today seem to have given up hope on the entire human race. Instead, let us, for a moment, contemplate what it means to be human.

In the whole history of the universe there has never been nor will there ever be again someone with exactly the same talents, passions, feelings, thoughts, experiences, abilities, mannerisms, brain, and body as another person. Even if a person were exactly the same in every way, even if they had the same DNA, they could not occupy that other person's physical space and would, by that very fact, be unique. Those of us who have known identical twins know this firsthand. Though, on the surface, they might look identical, though they possess the same DNA, they are different. There are subtleties in their appearance, mannerisms, experiences, abilities, talents, passions, and feelings that make them 100% unique. In this way, although we are all human, we are each completely unique. It truly is a miracle.

There's more. There's something deep within us, whether taught or inherited, that adds to our humanity. It goes by different names. Some call it "the high road." Some say "do unto others as you would have them do unto you." Some call it "do the right thing," "the 10 Commandments," "be nice," "do good," "empathy," or "love thy neighbor as thyself." Whatever it is, most people have it. Regardless of our behavior or outward action, conscience is there. It's the gentle tug. It's the sense of uneasiness down in our gut. It's the soft whisper that somehow tells us this is "right" and that is "wrong." It's that thing that makes us want to "**do something!**" It's the thing that keeps us up at night. It's what lets us differentiate between the hero and the villain. It's the "nudge," the "urge," the "discomfort" we have when we feel some injustice is being done. It's that soft little voice inside, the feeling we get in the pit of our stomach, the angel in our ear.

Whatever its source, we hear it, feel it, recognize it. Do other species have it? Hard to say. We can't really even prove it's there. Yet somehow it's there. At the end of the day we know it's there. We feel it even if we can't point to it. Where did it come from? What is it? It seems impossible that we, formed of matter, can feel it; yet, we feel it. It is the foundation of all religion, but a person does not need to be religious to identify it.

And yet society is blocking it out. "Modern life" is numbing it. Many cannot hear it above the alcohol, the drugs, the divisive political agendas, the television programming, the commercials, the peer pressure, the media stream, the gossip column, the "trying to change and control other people." Yet conscience, that ever illusive, mysterious, miraculous thing, is what connects us to our better selves as human beings.

The danger is that, with more than seven billion people on the planet today expected to grow to nine billion by 2050, it is more important than ever to listen to the voice. The challenge is that it is harder than ever to do it.

What is that voice? It's what urges Rick to tell Ilsa to leave with her husband Laslo at the end of the movie *Casablanca*. It's what makes all superheroes fight for justice. It's what makes a person donate a kidney to give another person a bit more time to live. It's what makes a student befriend the outcast at school. It's what makes a kid stick up for their sibling when they're being abused. It's what leads people to pause and consider how many children they can reasonably have and properly care for. In other words, it's knowing what's right and doing it. That's much harder than it sounds; yet, it is our calling. We are each called to be the hero of our own story.

There is something amazing about humans. It's even more amazing than the birds at the seabird sanctuary in Florida. It's even more amazing than the elephants that return to the graves of their loved ones each year. It's more amazing than Teddy the golden retriever who greets every four-legged creature as friend, and it's this: every person at every moment of every day has the potential to be a hero.

We are each the Artist of our own story. We each affect the sights, sounds, and sensations of the world around us at every moment of every day. We can fill our world with screams, violence, fear, neglect, abuse, impatience, and cruelty; or we can fill it with gratitude, peacefulness, hope, caring, love, intention, compassion, and kindness. Are we making good choices? Are we making good art?

With all our talent, with all our knowledge, with all our education, with all our potential, with all our conscience, and with seven billion people in the world today expected to grow to nine billion in 2050 we can certainly find a way to live more sustainably and harmoniously. If we cannot do this by looking to each other for guidance, let us at least look to nature. There is a simple example of this in nature. It's the true story about pelicans.

Pelicans have been looked at as the example of family life. If we pay attention we can observe this. Here is what happens. A junior pelican is very scared. It cannot traverse the open sea, and it is scared to leave the shore. The other birds are diving, searching for fish, and making their catch. The young pelican is weak and hungry. It stays close to shore. It doesn't know what to do. We observe that the other pelicans go out in search of the bird. What is it doing? Where is it? They circle. They go out, seeing if the young bird will join them. It is too scared. It remains. This goes on for quite some time. Then something very unusual happens. An elderly pelican, one far too old to be its parent, stays behind. It just stays close to the bird. It moves with it, dives with it, and imitates it. It does not leave its side. The rest of the flock periodically returns, but the senior bird stays close by. It does not leave. If the young bird tries to catch a fish, it does the same. If the bird swims and paddles around, the senior bird swims and paddles around. This goes on a very long time. It can take hours.

And then, finally, for some unknown reason, the junior bird and its senior mentor take off together to join the rest of the flock. The bird is not left to perish alone on the wide expanse of sea.

We are human. Our lower selves can be like dinosaurs. We can hate the other person because they are different. We can dismiss them because they don't do, think, or believe what we want. We can blow ourselves up with bombs, criticize one another, ignore our children, deplete our educational systems, destroy nature, treat each other as though we are not all part of the same human family; or we can be like the pelican, the elephant, the golden retriever, the hero, the one who takes time to listen to conscience and act accordingly. At every moment of every day, conscience is there. Can we hear it above the TV, above the gossip column, above the work schedule, the peer pressure, the evening news, the political agenda? Can we take time to answer our child's question? Can we visit the sick and aging? Can we invest more in education and the people who are passionate about educating? Can we take a brief moment to consider how many children we can reasonably love, sustain, and pay attention to, and then act accordingly?

With seven billion people in the world today expected to grow to nine billion by 2050 there is danger, but there is also endless opportunity.

Every age until now has conquered each other and nature. We are now a global society. If we continue to overpopulate, overconsume, destroy people, and destroy nature, we destroy ourselves.

Some people assert that the best way to escape the problems created by the Industrial Age is war—to blow ourselves up—thus destroying the unique contribution each person makes in the world. Have we learned nothing after two world wars and an atomic bomb? Did our conscience not resonate loud enough with those acts of violence? War is not the answer. It solves nothing. It only causes heartache and loss on both sides. Were war the answer, there would be no hunger, no poverty, no depression, no crime after two world wars. It doesn't even address the growth in population and consumption as the world's population and consumption increased (not decreased) after two world wars. Were war the answer, it certainly would not affect our conscience as it does. War is definitely not the answer.

War is an act of destruction. War is the base side of ourselves. War is the way of the dinosaur. War goes against conscience and religion and nature. War creates nothing.

The Artist hates war. The Artist does not want to see their work, their art, their legacy, their children, their sisters, their brothers, and themselves destroyed by it.

There are seven billion people on the planet. That number is expected to grow to nine billion by 2050. Can the beautiful planet Earth really sustain that kind of demand? We see the danger. We know what war, overpopulation, and overconsumption mean. We know there is terrible danger in them. We also know there is tremendous opportunity.

Our conscience is speaking, whispering at every moment of every day. Whether we evolved or were created does not matter.

The fact is that humans have more potential than any other species on the planet. At every moment of every day every person can do something heroic, no matter how seemingly small or insignificant. We can visit the elderly, smile at the cashier who is having a bad day, thank our teachers, overtip, be courteous to the other driver. We can take a brief moment to consider planning our family size based on our available talent, time, and resources. We can listen to our children, invest in their education, help others, give back to the planet that has so graciously given to us, and be grateful stewards of nature....

In other words we can use our prehistoric brain that is selfish, cruel, abusive, angry, dismissive, asleep, irresponsible, uncaring, lazy, and unaware; or we can use our Artist brain to be creative, inventive, encouraging, caring, alert, conscious, acting on our conscience for the good of nature and each other. We die as dinosaurs or live as Artists. With seven billion, the only way forward is to implore the better side of ourselves, to take the high road, to act with our conscience, to act with intention, to be the Artist.

Every age until now has been about conquering nature and each other. We're way beyond that. The way forward, the way to achieve the harmonious and sustainable coexistence of human beings among and within nature on this planet is so simple, so obvious, so easy to overlook, it's almost humorous. It's by imploring that most human of traits, the thing that whispers to us in the night, the thing that urges us to congregate at 5 p.m., remember our loved ones, and view even the most unlikely stranger as friend.

As the most evolved species, the stewards of the planet, with seven billion and counting, it's a great time:

> To be more family
>
> To be more mindful
>
> To be more golden

> To be a better Artist.

# CHAPTER 22

# DON'T QUIT BEFORE
# THE MIRACLE

....................

$M$any of us have heard the statement, "It would take a miracle to save the planet from the impending disaster." Miracle? Yes. Miracles are everywhere once we wake up to them, and so we can respond, "Don't quit before the miracle."

There are seven billion people on the planet. That number is expected to grow to nine billion by 2050. Overpopulation brings with it a great many sorrows. There is tremendous danger in it.

There is also tremendous opportunity.

With seven billion people right now, were each one to engage at every moment of every day in making the world a better place, just think of the potential that exists! Were each person to take an action to improve the state of the planet at some point in their lifetime, the world in which we live, a planet which sustains our lives, which is more beautiful, alive, and varied beyond anything we could ever hope for or imagine, just think of what might be possible! Were each person to experience and express that gratitude through their own talent it would have a tremendous impact. It could be in the planting of a grove of trees, the cleaning of a local river, the design of an improved building model, the support of a sustainable energy source, the practice of responsible and voluntary family planning, the advocacy of diversity and stewardship, the education of youth in becoming responsible planetary stewards,.... Each action has value and meaning, and each person at each moment of each day has the great potential to make the world in which we live a better place.

Sometimes we feel stuck. Our lives seem limited. It seems we have no choice, that our lives are on default mode and we are stuck forever in the sensory deprivation/overload chamber. The Artist is no prisoner to modern life. The Artist sees opportunity. The Artist wakes up to the senses. The Artist wakes up to their talents. The Artist realizes the tremendous importance of each action regardless of how small it might seem. We are each an Artist of the world we inhabit. We can act and think in a way that makes the world a little better than we left it. In the end, that is our calling in life.

Seven billion people. Seven billion actions.

That is a lot of influence. More than ever before.

There is danger. There is opportunity.

The greatest moment in human history will be when we embrace the opportunity that seven billion actions present, when all citizens begin communicating, innovating, and working together toward a common goal, which is the harmonious and sustainable coexistence of human beings among and within nature on this planet.

We are all standing on the cusp of that great moment, the moment when we each recognize our calling as grateful stewards and human beings inhabiting the most beautiful, varied, and awesome planet we have ever known or will know, the moment when we each express gratitude toward each other and recognize the miracle of planet Earth.

The Industrial Age was good but not great. At the beginning of it the planet was teeming with life, varied and beautiful. Sustaining such varied and beautiful life requires taking the next step. We are entering a New Age, an age when we, as Artists, begin to innovate, to think differently, to integrate, and most of all, to care. We can live in default mode, continue the Industrial Age, and do nothing, or we can embrace the opportunity to improve the quality of life for the current generation of citizens and all future inhabitants of planet Earth.

Stewardship is a most noble and ethical art. To recognize, appreciate, and respect the miracle is an awesome privilege and responsibility.

# CHAPTER 23

# THE ARTIST'S CALLING

...................

"If we did all the things we are capable of,
we would literally astound ourselves."

*—Thomas Edison, Inventor and Artist*

Imagine that you are sitting under the night sky. It is a new moon, and you are far from civilization. The sky is a thick black velvet of empty space. As you lie on your back looking up at the backdrop of space, seven billion stars appear. Each star radiates in a different hue, each with a different intensity, each in a different position. The stars blink, each at its own rate. Though different, each looks like a precious jewel on the velvet backdrop of the night sky.

Now imagine that each of the seven billion stars is a person, each one created unique and bestowed with individual talents. Some have a talent for language, others for humor, others for building. Some have talents for carpentry, painting, teaching, writing, repair, listening, parenting, gardening, etc. As you gaze upon them you realize that they are not limited to one talent only but that they are bestowed with multiple talents. Imagine that the more talent, the brighter the light from that star so that as you gaze upon them they become brighter and brighter, overflowing with the intensity of their realized potential, which is to create and do good works. The greater the talent, the brighter the star.

Now take a moment to contemplate the planet: its air, water, vegetation, animals, the great variety of life. What is the quality of the air? What is the quality of the water? What is happening to the animals, vegetation, and variety of that life? You did not create it. It was here long before civilization, before language, before human beings. Imagine the contrast of the blank expanse of the great dark universe in comparison to the precious animated living planet.

As you look at the great potential of the seven billion and the current condition of the planet, is it beyond reason to suppose that if each soul were to value the diversity of life on this planet and work toward its betterment using the great diversity of talent with which each was bestowed, the planet would be both beautiful and sustainable for all future generations?

The Artist is a sensitive, creative, innovative, talented, and hardworking being. The Artist lives an intentional life, performing intentional works. Each person who has lived, is living, and ever will live is an Artist. At its core, it is what separates us from other living things: our ability to shape the world in which we live. This includes both how we treat each other and how we treat the planet.

The Artist is not perfect, but the Artist is not seeking perfection, only progress, slow, steady progress toward a goal. There is no one way to be an Artist. Not all people were intended to be painters, parents, carpenters, sculptors, linguists, or chefs. Artists recognize and appreciate the great beauty and variety of life, of people, of talents, of professions, and occupations. There is no one way to be an Artist, no singular requirement for creating art. Age, gender, race, nationality, language, marital status, "generation," intelligence, income, political affiliation, health, religion, etc., neither qualify nor exclude one from becoming an Artist. Art is an equal opportunity occupation.

Humans have unlimited capacity to do good. We are the bright stars in the night sky. This world in which we live is the greatest miracle we will ever know in our lifetimes.

The moment when we all treasure it as Artists and work toward its betterment as Artists will be the greatest moment in human history.

# APPENDIX A:
# QUESTIONS

## Chapter 12: The Miracle of the Cycle of Life

- What is the ratio of empty space (parking lots, empty fields, large buildings, etc.) to natural habitat in your area?

- Are there any areas that you observe which are vacant that have the potential to be artistically redesigned in favor of nature?

- What would be the benefit of creating a nature habitat in your yard?

- What talents could you contribute to redesigning your city to make it more beautiful and nature-friendly?

- What actions could you take to advocate for a local park or nature preserve?

## Chapter 13: The Miracle of the Tree

- What opportunities do you see for planting trees in your yard, neighborhood, city, and state?

- What do you currently observe happening to the trees in your area?

- What ways can you think of that trees benefit humans?

- What ways can you think of that humans can benefit trees?

- What is one action you could take in your lifetime in this area?

## Chapter 14: The Miracle of the Animal

- Did you ever teach your child the story of Noah's Ark?

- What opportunities are there for social media to communicate the status of animals around the globe?

- What is one action you could take to support a zoo or nature preserve?

- What is one action you could take to advocate for animals in jeopardy of becoming extinct for the rest of eternity?

- If you could release animals back into the wild like Noah did, where would you put them?

## Chapter 15: The Miracle of Peace and Quiet

- What eye, ear, nose, tongue, and tactile pollution do you observe in your neighborhood?

- How much time (if any) do you take every day to focus on something beautiful?

- What opportunities exist in your area to clean up visual, auditory, tactile, and olfactory pollution?

- If you could make one improvement in this area in your lifetime, what would it be?

- Would you ever consider signing a petition, voting, picketing, writing, or even running for office to make a positive difference in this area?

## Chapter 16: The Miracle of Simplicity

- Did you ever "sleepwalk" your way through a day? What did this feel like?

- What is your favorite memory? What was happening? Who was there? What were you doing?

- If you could change one thing in your life to make it more simple, what would it be?

- Do you ever feel like life is too busy, too stressful, or too complex?

- What are the seemingly "important" things in your life you are doing today that are taking the place of things that are truly important and meaningful?

## Chapter 17: The Miracle of All Natural

- What can you do to advocate for cleaner, safer, fresher food and water?

- What do you observe in relation to bees, insects, birds, and wildlife in your area?

- What choices do you feel you have as a consumer and an employee in advocating for better, safer, healthier methods in relation to food and water?

- What does organic and all natural mean to you?

- What impact do you think organic and natural have on your family's life and health?

## Chapter 18: The Miracle of Bees and Wasps

- What do you think John Muir meant when he said "when we tug on a single thing in nature we find it attached to everything else"?

- What changes do you observe in your area that are impacting bees, flowers, plants, trees, insects, and birds?

- What ways can you think of that bees, wasps, and other insects benefit humans?

- What ways can you think of that humans can benefit bees, wasps, and other insects?

- What is one thing you could do in your lifetime to make a positive impact in this area?

## Chapter 19: The Miracle of a Sustainable Climate

- What changes have you observed in relation to climate in the last 20 years?

- What opportunities do you observe for cleaning up your neighborhood, city, state, and country?

- What impact do you think a clean or dirty planet has on children?

- What is one thing you could do in your lifetime to make an impact in this area?

- When you are working toward the betterment of the planet, do you associate your actions with leadership?

## Chapter 20: The Miracle of the Senses

- Have you ever lived in the sensory deprivation/overload chamber? If so, what did it feel like?

- What do you think a person can do to get out of the sensory deprivation/overload chamber?

- What are your favorite sensory experiences today?

- What senses do you engage the most?

- What senses could you engage more in order to live more fully?

## Chapter 21: The Miracle of Conscience

- What can you do to be more golden, more mindful, and more family oriented?

- How can you personally contribute to greater harmony and sustainability in the world?

- What responsibility do people who have or intend to have children have in regard to nature and the environment?

- How is responsible and voluntary family planning linked to increased harmony and sustainability in the world?

- Taking into account the global population, what does responsible and voluntary family planning mean to you?

## Chapter 22: Don't Give Up Before the Miracle

- As you contemplate all of the opportunity in today's world, what hope do you see for the future?

- What do you think "human beings among and within nature on this planet" looks like?

- If you could create a movie of the future that showed a happy picture of people and nature, what would the planet look like?

- What do the terms *stewardship* and *sustainability* mean to you?

- What opportunities do you have this very day to make a positive difference in the world?

## Chapter 23: The Artist's Calling

- What types of art (intentional acts to bring vision into the world) are you capable of?

- In what ways do you acknowledge the unique and precious contribution you bring into the world?

- What opportunities do you have to make the planet a better place to live through your time, talent, and treasure?

- If you could do one thing in your lifetime to make the world a better, healthier, cleaner, more beautiful place to live, what would it be?

- What are you waiting for?

# APPENDIX B:
# ONE PERSON CAN
# MAKE A DIFFERENCE!

## Simple Things Every Person Can Do to Make the World a Better Place

- Turn off lights when you leave a room
- Power down idle electronics
- Use compact florescent lightbulbs
- Adjust thermostat two degrees
- Install proper insulation and seals
- Replace old dishwashers with newer models
- Use microwaves instead of ovens
- Buy appliances with the Energy Saver rating
- Use attic fans instead of AC on cool days
- Buy cars that get 32 miles per gallon or better
- Raise lawn mower blades
- Bring your lunch to the office
- Advocate for public transportation
- Share the road with cyclists and small vehicles
- Sign up for electronic bill pay
- Print on both sides of the paper
- Unsubscribe from junk mail lists
- Bring your own grocery bags
- Use the recycle bin at work and at home
- Support small farmers and local growers
- Reduce food consumption
- Eat natural foods over processed ones

- Fix leaky faucets
- Replace old toilets with newer models
- Drink tap water over bottled water
- Take shorter, more temperate showers
- Plant a tree to reduce atmospheric $CO_2$
- Prune trees instead of topping/chopping
- Visit and sponsor parks and nature preserves
- Avoid pesticides
- Use organic fertilizer
- Plant native trees and flowers when possible
- Plant fruit trees and flowering plants
- Encourage pollinators like bees and butterflies
- Teach children to respect and appreciate nature
- Teach children to act responsibly
- Encourage children to play outside
- Practice responsible family planning
- Advocate for education
- Advocate for sustainability programs in schools
- Teach children to save money and energy
- Promote art and nature in schools and at home
- Use social media to encourage more ideas
- Use social media to encourage action
- Use books and websites to learn more
- Donate to your favorite organization
- Share information and ideas like these with friends and coworkers

## ACKNOWLEDGMENTS

Thanks to my many family members and friends
for their ongoing support and encouragement.
You all mean the world to me.


Special thanks go out to
Dane (friend, sounding board, and editor)
Jewel, Beth, and Jennifer
(dear friends, educators, and mentors)

# ABOUT THE AUTHOR

Katherine Maria Pinner lives in St. Louis, Missouri, where she works as an organizational development consultant, implementing innovative and technical business solutions in a way that unleashes human potential. She holds numerous professional certifications in her field. She earned a Bachelor of Arts in Literature and a Master of Arts in English. Her greatest passions are for public speaking, writing, education, and the environment.